Eat Now; Talk Later

Eat Now; Talk Later

52 True Tales of Family, Feasting, and the American Dream

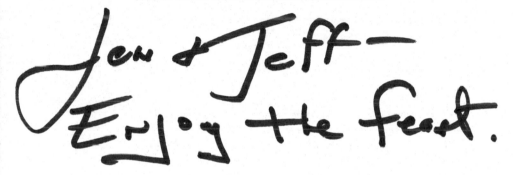

Jen & Jeff —
Enjoy the feast.

JAMES VESCOVI

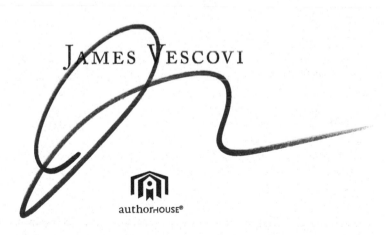

authorHOUSE®

AuthorHouse™ LLC
1663 Liberty Drive
Bloomington, IN 47403
www.authorhouse.com
Phone: 1-800-839-8640

Published by AuthorHouse 12/30/2013

ISBN: 978-1-4918-3148-9 (sc)
ISBN: 978-1-4918-3149-6 (e)

Library of Congress Control Number: 2013920306

This book is printed on acid-free paper.

Some of these stories have appeared in a slightly different form in the following publications: The New York Times, New York Newsday, Ancestry magazine, Creative Nonfiction, Alimentum: The Literature of Food, and La Gazetta Italiana, as well in the anthologies Avanti Popolo and Memories of Our Grandparents.

TABLE OF CONTENTS

For my Father,
with love and respect

and with thanks to family and friends
for their encouragement

and a special thanks
to Cynthia Zarin,
who first urged me to write
these tales down.

INTRODUCTION

This collection of stories began with my father, Selvi. His career as a pharmaceutical executive took him around the world, and he returned home with amazing stories. Moreover, he was a born storyteller with a great sense of timing, a true *raconteur*. I heard my first story one evening when members of my parents' Bridge group took a break between rubbers, and he regaled them with this gem.

He'd just returned from a two-week trip to Milan, Italy, and, on the weekend in between, he had visited the remote mountain village were his father, Antonio, had grown up. The place is called Casaselvatica, and it is located thirty miles southwest of the city of Parma, which is eighty miles north of Florence and eighty miles south of Milan.

He stayed with his Uncle Domenico, my grandfather's younger brother, who still lived in the family house. They drank wine and talked about former days. They looked at old photos. There were visits from townspeople, friends of my grandfather, who came to scrutinize his American son.

By Sunday noon, my father said good-bye and drove to a nearby town called Berceto to buy dried *funghi*, or mushrooms, for which the area is known. They were for my mother who, living in the Midwest in the 1970s, found it difficult, if not impossible, to buy ingredients to cook Italian. After making his purchase, he took a stroll and had an espresso and finally got into his rental car for the three-hour trip to Milan.

As he put the key in the ignition, an old woman, dressed in black, came out from the shadows of the town's ninth-century cathedral, and approached his window.

"*Signore*, are you by any chance heading towards the Autostrada?" she asked, in Italian. The Autostrada is a series of highways that covers the country.

"*Sì,*" he said. "Yes."

She sighed. "I wonder if you wouldn't give me a ride," she said. "As you can see, I am an old woman. I came to Berceto to do some marketing"—here she lifted up some parcels she was carrying—"and I just missed my bus. This is Sunday, and the next one won't leave for five hours."

"I'd be happy to give you a ride," my father said. He climbed out, placed her packages in the trunk, and helped her in the car.

"My village is called Fugazzolo," she said. My father knew it. It was where his parents had married.

They were soon driving on a winding, two-lane road. The old woman made small talk and my father responded, though his mind was on business he'd do that week. He noticed that the woman, as she chatted away, was looking intently at him. He figured it was because he was a stranger in these parts, and even though they were speaking Italian, strangers always came under scrutiny.

Finally, she broke the tension and said, "And what is a gentleman from Milano doing in a small town like Berceto?"

My father laughed. "I'm an American. I'm in Milano on business," he said.

"That's even more interesting," she said. "What is an American doing in these parts?"

"I'm visiting family," my father replied.

After a long pause, the woman remarked, "Isn't that wonderful when you Americans can come over to this side and see the way your people lived and taste the culture. Wonderful."

They drove a few more miles. Small talk ceased. The car got quiet. The craggy-faced woman continued to stare at him. Her eyes went up and down, raking his features, absorbing their every detail. My father cleared his throat and made a comment about the weather, but was feeling uncomfortable.

She said, "I don't mean to pry into your business, but I am very curious. I have lived in these parts for my entire life. Who is it you were visiting?"

"Domenico Vescovi, from Casaselvatica," my father replied. "He's my uncle."

She nodded. "I know him—not very well, mind you, but I know who he is. There are so few people around here that we all know one another. Domenico Vescovi, yes."

Once again, her eyes fell on my father, and the car filled with silence. Minutes later they entered Fugazzolo, a small cluster of houses perched on a mountainside. The woman pointed out her house and my father headed towards it.

As he downshifted the gears, she sighed and said, "I really don't mean to pry into your business, but if I don't ask you this question I will never forgive myself."

They pulled up in front of her door, and the car jerked to a halt.

By now, my father had had enough of this mystery. He wanted to know who she was and what all the scrutiny was about. He laughed and said, "Please, ask."

She took a deep breath. "Well, you say that Domenico Vescovi is your uncle?"

"Yes."

"Would you by any chance have been acquainted with his brother, the one who emigrated to the United States, Antonio Vescovi?"

"Of course I would," said my father, with a smile, "he is my father."

She pointed a bony finger at him and said, "And I should have been your mother!"

For a moment, my father felt as if she were making some kind of a joke, but, no, she had taken his hands into hers. Her eyes were twinkling. "*Si, e vero,*" she said. "It's true.

"*Allora, Milano può aspettare.* Milano can wait," she added. "*Viene a casa, prendiamo un caffe.* Come in for some coffee."

Like a number of women in those hills sixty years earlier, this woman had had eyes for Tony. He was strong and handsome, she said, and he had a beautiful singing voice. After coming home from World War I, he left for America. The signora waited three years for him to return then married someone else

My father laughed all the way back to Milano. The woman lived on one side of Antonio's village, while my grandmother had lived far on the other. He must have been a busy man, riding his bike back and forth between sweethearts.

A few weeks later, my father had lunch with his parents. He waited for his mother Desolina to clear the dishes and go to the kitchen. Then he said, "So, Pa, I was in Italy and met someone who asked me to pass along her greetings."

"Yeah?" Tony asked, without much interest. "Qui?"

Hearing about my father's visits to Italy was bittersweet for him. Now eighty, there was a part of him that felt antiquated and out of place in America, but returning to the old country would have dredged up too many sad memories of the farm and the struggles and the face of his blessed mother.

My father said the woman's name.

Tony's jaw started to drop, but he fought it back up. With his hand, he chopped the air, signaling that all conversation should cease. He put an index finger to his lips and motioned to the front door. They threw on their coats and went outside

Anything Tony had done with this woman, whether respectable or not, would have occurred long ago, but he wasn't taking chances. Desolina was a very possessive woman.

It was a warm spring day, and they walked slowly down the sidewalk while my father recounted the tale. Tony's Fedora was perched on his head, its brim angled low. Had you faced him with your back to the sun, a shadow would've covered his face.

The story ended. Tony halted. He turned. He raised the brim of his hat. His eyes met my father's.

"*É ancora bella?*" he asked. "Is she still good-looking?"

And from this story came many others about Tony and Desolina, including some that I myself have carefully collected.

It would be impossible to tell the story of my grandparents through a traditional biography. They were not famous and did nothing that we might deem extraordinary, like invent a successful product or argue a seminal case before the U.S. Supreme Court. Instead, like most of us, they lived quiet, anonymous lives. Yet, how do we tell others about our great grandmother who lived in a sod hut on the plains of South Dakota, or our Uncle Buck, who took part in the arrest of a famous bank robber?

Most often, it is through stories. For example, how did that woman in the sod hut feed her children during the winter after her husband died of pneumonia? What were your Uncle Buck's thoughts when walked out of his hotel in Hurley, Wisconsin, in 1935, and saw the robber seated in a car scrutinizing the local bank? Or, in the case of my grandmother, an Italian immigrant who ate only Italian food her entire life, what was it like to watch her try McDonald's Quarter Pounders, fries, and shakes when she was past ninety? Or to sit with my grandfather who, when he had to be hospitalized in 1991, pulled $1,000 in cash from under his pajamas to pay the bill?

I heard and experienced dozens of stories like these, which I shared among family, friends, and colleagues—even strangers. Largely, listeners enjoyed them—laughed, teared up, or shook their heads in wonder—because these tales had a universal quality about them. What person, no matter how anonymously he or she lived, does not yield unique tales that tell us about character, history—in short, about what it is to be human?

The most difficult task in writing this book was not recording the stories, but finding the best way to organize them. I decided to divide them into five thematic categories, which represent the essence of who Tony and Desolina Vescovi were and how they lived.

They are *Sagra, Stati uniti, Semplicitá, Si Ricordiamo,* and *Stare per finire.*

The *sagra* was an annual village feast dedicated to a local saint, when impoverished peasants like my grandparents ate and drank like kings and queens. This chapter contains stories about food. To Desolina, making conversation during a meal was like shouting during a church sermon. It was forbidden. Anyone who attempted speak during a meal was told, "Eat now; talk later." To my grandparents, eating was paramount, even sacred.

Stati uniti is Italian for United States. Tony immigrated here in 1922, went back to Italy seven years later to marry, and returned in 1930 with his pregnant wife. Here you will find tales about my grandparents' appreciation and often humorous misunderstanding of all things American.

Tony was born in 1899, Desolina twenty-five days after the turn of the century. They were creatures of a medieval mindset because they'd been born into a farming culture that hadn't much changed in hundreds of years—hence the title of the third section, *Semplicitá,* (Simplicity). The stories here are bittersweet, as you might expect with people living during an era and in a culture they never understood.

Si ricordiamo means, roughly, "We remember". Here stories about my grandparents' youth are juxtaposed with stories about visits my father and I made to their villages fifty or more years later and the things we discovered about them.

Finally, *stare per finire*—"the beginning of the end." Tony lived until he was ninety-three, Desolina until she was ninety-six. These fiercely independent folks did not go gently into the good night. Caring for them during their final years with dignity called for sacrifice, creativity, and some hocus-pocus.

I hope you enjoy these stories. More importantly, I hope they help you recall reminiscences of your own grandparents, second cousins, and crazy aunts that you can pass down through your own families.

For Italian speakers, please note that the Italian phrases in the book are in my grandparents' local dialect and in standard Italian because they used both.

La Sagra

The Feast

In America, every day is a feast day.
Tony (far left) and Desolina (far right)
enjoy a meal with family in the late 1950s.

TO ASTORIA

It was 1967. I was seven. We drove all night. My mother was asleep in the front seat, her head cocked back on the headrest. My younger sister was belted and tucked into the middle seat. My brother and I were in the back of the station wagon, whose seats had been flattened to make a platform, upon which we dozed under blankets knitted by my grandmother Desolina, whom we were going to see.

It was nearly impossible to sleep during these rides. The motion of the car and the hum of our tires did nothing to lull me into slumber. I watched my father's steady hands on the steering wheel. Occasionally, one reached below for a cup of coffee. His squarish head was silhouetted by passing semis; his window was cracked to give him a flow of fresh air into the heated car.

I eventually fell asleep but was awakened a few hours later by the rattling of change as my father paid the toll collector on the Pennsylvania Turnpike. The sun rose. We stopped for breakfast. Two hours later, we arrived in Astoria, Queens, New York, 700 miles from our home in Kalamazoo, Michigan. Before my father had thrown the Ford Esquire into park, I burst out of the car and, with my siblings at my heels, raced up the stoop and into the vestibule of 34-44 30ᵗʰ Street.

I pressed the bell. The wait lasted only a few seconds but seemed interminable. The door buzzed loudly, like an obnoxious alarm clock, but to us it was music. It meant the lock was disengaged, and we shoved open the door and raced down the hallway, its walls sculpted with tin *fleur-de-lis*. We ran up the stairs, two steps at a time. By the second floor, I could already smell the scent of mothballs that pervaded my grandparents' apartment. A door opened on the floor above us. That was Desolina and my grandfather, Tony, standing next to the dumbwaiter. When they saw us, they clapped their hands. Tears sparkled in their eyes.

Desolina slobbered us with kisses.

"*Tesoro della Nonna! Tes-O-ro della Nonna!*" she said. "Grandmother's treasure."

My grandfather embraced us with his workingman's arms. We jumped up and down. The light from the skylight over the staircase always seemed extra bright.

Desolina hurried us inside while Tony went downstairs to greet my parents and help with luggage. My grandparents lived in a two-bedroom apartment in a small, three-story building. They spent most of their time in one room where they ate and watched TV and where Tony slept at night on a pull out couch. The table was covered in plastic, and a glass cabinet held china and espresso cups that they rarely used and a bottle of whiskey from which my grandfather took an occasional morning snort. The walls were bare except for a photo of my grandfather during World War I, when he served as a member of crack marksmen known as *Bersagliere*. He is wearing his dress uniform, which included a wide-brimmed hat pierced by a decorative ostrich-feather. The only other thing on the walls were Band-Aids pasted here and there to keep paint cracks from expanding.

My siblings and I raced around the apartment like dogs that needed to sniff familiar places. First stop: the aluminum breadbox in the kitchen. Yes! Stocked with marshmallow cookies we could not get in Michigan. We darted into the second bedroom and opened the lid on a glass covered dish: plenty of gum and Life Savers. We went into their bedroom to look at their wedding day portrait: Tony hadn't much changed, but Desolina had. Her black hair had turned gray and her arms and chin now swayed with friendly flesh.

We poked our heads into the refrigerator to see whether Desolina had made tortellini. Again, yes! There were hundreds. Soon, Tony and my parents appeared, huffing and puffing, with the luggage.

The first order of business: sit down and eat. We planted ourselves around the long kitchen table, where a platter of prosciutto, salami, capponata, and cheese had been laid out. The crust of the fresh-baked bread from the pizzeria cracked when we broke it into sandwich lengths. My brother dug out the fluffy white, shaped it into a communion wafer, and slipped it on his tongue. We made sandwiches and began stuffing ourselves.

After the antipasti, Desolina served up heaping bowls of tortellini in brodo. The homemade hats of dough and stuffing were not completely air tight, so that when you bit into one you got a squirt of warm broth.

Everyone stuffed himself to capacity. Nothing was said; no news was exchanged at the table. If you tried, Desolina would say, "Eat now; talk later."

There were no leftovers either. If there were three slices of salami or a ladle-full of tortellini remaining, Tony put it away. He was all muscle, not an ounce of fat. He liked his tortellini *brodoso*, with a lot of broth. When he disposed of the tortellini, he poured red wine into the broth, picked up the bowl, and drank. I watched him in wonderment.

None of my friends had grandparents like these. Theirs looked simply like older versions of their parents. Tony and Desolina were exotic. They spoke a strange dialect of Italian. Vowels could sometimes plummet to the guttural depths of German. They drank wine at lunch and at supper. They didn't drive and never would. Desolina was always in a dress and kerchief and, underneath, a girdle with a million snaps. I used to listen to her undo them at night: It sounded like Houdini getting out of a straitjacket. Tony wore a Fedora and his woolen shirts up to his neck, even in summer. He mixed his own shave cream, used a straight razor, and never shaved without a lit cigar in his mouth. They looked like black licorice sticks and their odor infused my hair. In their bedroom was a huge, broad faced alarm clock whose bells sounded like those at a fire station. Their wedding photo resembled the tinted photos of Abe Lincoln. When they walked, the apartment floor creaked beneath them.

Tony and Desolina had arrived in America during the 1920s. Back in Italy, each village had a *sagra*, a yearly festival dedicated to a saint. It was a kind of potlatch in which each family went all out in preparing a feast. A pig was slaughtered by a professional butcher, who was paid with a choice piece of pork. Anything that wasn't consumed at the *sagra* was made into salami. On this day, you ate like the *padrone*, the rich landowner himself. I once asked Tony what he liked best about America. Was it opportunity for himself and his children? Access to good health care? While he valued these things, he replied, "Because in America I eat every day like it's the *sagra*."

WHERE'S THE HUDSON?

In 1983, I moved to New York to attend graduate school. On Saturday mornings, while my friends were sleeping off hangovers, I took a 40-minute subway ride to Astoria. At noon, when my friends were eating Eggs Benedict at the latest hot brunch spot and talking about sports or getting laid, I was eating Mortadella wrapped around Stella Doro breadsticks and listening to my grandfather tell the story about the time he almost beat up the local garlic seller for spreading false rumors about my father stealing his mail. The antipasti was followed by ravioli, fruit, and some dessert, usually a boxed pie or vanilla ice cream. The rest of the afternoon until about 4:30 was taken up with sitting on the stoop and playing cards. After that, we'd eat again.

My grandparents liked Astoria. In the mid-1950s, my father had convinced them to move because their current neighborhood in Manhattan, Hell's Kitchen, had grown seedy and dangerous with the expansion of a bus terminal. Astoria was a neighborhood of tree-lined streets, small apartment houses, and a respectable working-class population of Poles, Slavs, and Italians. John's Delicatessen on Broadway, a main thoroughfare (but not the famous Broadway that travels the length of Manhattan), offered everything Tony and Desolina wanted: prosciutto di Parma, cheese, olives, torrone, and, at Christmas, fresh Panetone. Broadway also had a Jewish restaurant, a Polish butcher, and plenty of Irish bars, but my grandparents walked past those places; they were for the other people in the neighborhood.

One torrid Saturday afternoon I went to the C-Town supermarket to do Tony and Desi's shopping. My grandmother's handwriting was getting worse. I thought I had found all the items she wanted, but left the store with an uneasy feeling.

I entered their sweltering apartment to find the fan that I had set up had been unplugged and put away. Desolina insisted that fan breezes, even on a 98-degree day, could cause respiratory problems. Forget about air conditioning. They kept themselves cool by wearing light wool, which turns the body's cooling system on by heating up just a little, and sitting still as wax figures.

I sloughed into the kitchen, my t-shirt sticking to my sweaty back. I began unloading groceries. The hallway linoleum creaked with slow, heavy foot steps.

Desolina appeared. I'd left the change and receipt on a counter, which was the requisite policy. She stuffed the money and receipt in her apron pocket. Whether she ever checked them to see if I'd short-changed her I don't know.

She poked her nose into the bags.

"*Dove il gelato?*" she asked. "Where's the ice cream?"

That's what I had forgotten!

Desolina couldn't get enough of vanilla ice cream. She'd take a heaping portion, chopped up until it was the consistency of soft serve, and went at it like a cat with cream.

Did she really expect me to go back outside, where the sidewalks were baking at 120 degrees and not a breeze had blown for the past forty-eight hours?

She pulled a few bucks out of her apron and planted them in my hand.

As I went out, she called out, "See Jimmy? *Se non si usa la testa, si usa le gambe.* If you don't use your head, you end up using your legs." She chuckled.

Desolina could be quite impatient with me. As we sat down one day to *tortellini* in *brodo*, she discovered she'd forgotten a ladle.

"*Jimmy, vai prendre il mestolo.*"

I got up and trooped down to the kitchen. Tony and Desolina had more ladles than screwdrivers in a hardware store: big, small, metal, copper. I picked one from a utensil drawer and returned.

Desolina rolled her eyes.

"*No, il mestolo grande,*" she said. "The big ladle."

I huffed back to the kitchen, dug through the drawer. As far as I could see, I had found the largest one and brought it to the table.

She slapped her forehead.

"Jimmy, c'mon, *il mestolo* that we use every time we have tortellini."

"Well, where it is it?!" I asked, testily.

"In the kitchen," she replied.

"I know, but where?!"

"In the pot on the stove."

Why did it matter? I asked myself as I stormed back to the kitchen. Big, small, tall, short. By this time we all could have eaten two bowls of soup.

I opened the oven, which Desolina used for storage. There it was, a big pot, with two enamel ladles. Had they been animate, they could have been identical twins. I held them up, examined their length and diameter. The only difference was a tiny dent. I came back with the other one.

When Desolina saw it, she gave me a glare that could've melted lead. She got up from the table, tottered down to the kitchen, and returned with the twin.

She ladled out the tortellini. My face was red with a mixture of anger and shame.

She sat down. She picked up her spoon and said, "Don't get married, Jimmy. You're too stupid . . . . you're so stupid, you couldn't find the Hudson from here if you walked west."

Tony found it so funny that broth dribbled down his chin.

ON THE BOAT

I got married in 1987 on a brilliant September evening—absolutely perfect for the reception, which was a three-hour dinner cruise around New York Harbor.

The ship set sail, the bar opened, and everyone was having a good time, though my father considered himself "on duty." He knew that Tony, whose doctor permitted him only an occasional drink, would attempt to tie one on. Desolina also needed special attention because she had no idea she was on a boat. She sometimes got confused when she was out of her usual environment, even though she'd been escorted across a gangplank. To her, the boat could have been a small restaurant with a view of the Hudson River.

My grandparents were positioned in two captain's chairs in the main salon, while my father and others went back and forth to the buffet tables to bring them what they wanted. Occasionally, he was called away for a photo or in his duties as father of the groom. Tony capitalized on this opportunity to celebrate beyond the one-drink limit, using my friends as gofers. Most had never met my grandparents and went up to say hello.

"Mr. Vescovi, I'm Gary, a friend of Jim's. He's told me all about you. Congratulations."

"Thank you very much," my grandfather said.

"It's a beautiful evening, isn't it?" said the friend, pointing to the full moon.

"*Perfetto*," my grandfather said.

And then Gary, wanting to be of service to an elderly man, said, "Is there anything I can get for you?"

"Scotch."

"O.K., I'll be right back."

As Gary walked off, Tony yelled, "Make it a double!"

9

Drinks were served by Gary and Robert. Steve brought a third. My father kept coming back to the salon to find his father a little more in the bag. Desolina wasn't noticing anything. She had guests serving her more prime rib, salad, and bread.

"Very nice people," she said of my friends.

The party continued. We sailed past the Statue of Liberty, and my grandfather slouched towards a window and looked proudly on the Old Dame. We cruised under the Brooklyn Bridge. The voice of Ella Fitzgerald crooned over the sound system. Bulbs flashed. People laughed. The cake came out.

By 11 p.m., Desolina had eaten her fill and was ready to depart for home. She signaled my father over to her chair.

"*Andiamo*," she said. "Let's go."

"*Andiamo?*" asked my father. There was still an hour left in the cruise. "We can't go."

"Oh, no," she said. "I know the young people want to stay and celebrate some more. That's right and good. But me, I'm an old woman and I want to go home. *Sono stanca*. I'm tired." She pointed to Tony, who was nodding off. "*Andiamo*, Selvi."

"But, Mama, we can't go," said my father.

"*Perche no?*" she asked indignantly.

"*Semma in barca*," he replied. "We're on a boat."

"*Na barca?!*" she asked, looking at him as if he'd had more drinks than Tony. "*Sei mato*. You're crazy. C'mon, *andiamo!*" she added, getting to her feet.

My father brought her over to the window and pointed out how the lights of New York City were moving by.

"See, we're on a boat!" he said.

Desolina marveled at the notion. "*Una barca!*"

She looked around at the ship's appointments, turned to my father, and said "*É bella questa barca*. This is a beautiful boat."

She sighed and shrugged. My father led her back to her chair. There was nothing else for her to do except eat more wedding cake.

PIZZA

Everyone thinks Italians eat pizza all the time but it wasn't so in my family. If Tony and Desolina ate pizza twenty times in their 90+ years I would be surprised. My grandmother was suspicious of any food that she didn't prepare in her own kitchen. No hotdogs or macaroni and cheese. No turkey. Chocolate was considered bad for you, even in bite-size amounts.

As a boy, the only pizza my father ate was given to him by Anna Lanza, the pudgy woman who lived next door. Anna's husband was a waiter at Sardi's and was gone six nights a week. He didn't come home until the wee hours of the morning, and Anna got lonely. During the evening, she played loud Italian music, drank beer, and danced around her apartment with a broom. At the end of each song, she stepped on the bristles and slammed down the broom, which caused my grandfather to yell, "*Porco cane! Basta, Anna!*"

("*Porco cane*" was Tony's favorite curse. Literally, it means "pig dog." The word *porco* is often attached to other nouns by Italians to generate curses, such as "*porca vaca*" (pig cow) and "*porca putana*" (pig slut). Anything will do.)

As my grandparents got older, their culinary orthodoxy abated. I guess they saw their lives coming to a close and figured, "So what if this Hershey Bar kills me? I'm 90 years old." They began to try new foods, though only if I brought them into their home. I thought it was pathetic that they had tried so little of the great variety of cuisine New York offers. With the exception of post-funeral dinners, they never ate out.

There was a second reason why I'd begun to bring in meals. My grandfather, who did most of the cooking in his latter years, had begun to boil the hell out of pasta. It was 20 minutes past *al dente*, practically a pulp you would give to an infant. I couldn't understand it. His teeth were still good. Why was he cooking the linguine into such mush? I would go into the kitchen—the water had been boiling for so long the room felt like a sauna—and pull out a strand to taste it.

"*Nonno, e pronta.* It's ready."

He would wag his finger at me and say, "*No. Due o tre minuti ancora,* two or three minutes more."

I looked in the pot. The water looked pasty. It made my stomach turn. But what could I do? He was 90, and I wasn't going to argue with him.

When the bowl of pasta came to the table I could hardly touch it. Even my grandmother, who ate anything, complained.

One day, no longer able to stand eating enervated pasta, I called ahead before one of my weekly visits to announce that I was bringing lunch. Tony, who didn't like anyone spending money on him, was nevertheless getting old and tired and demurred.

After getting off the subway in Astoria, I passed Phil's Jewish Delicatessen. That seemed as good a place as any to start. I showed up at their apartment with franks and beans, potato salad, and cream soda. The meal was a hit. There wasn't a bean left in sight, and Desolina told me that whenever I passed by Phil's to be sure to buy her quarter pound of potato salad.

The following Saturday I got pizza, followed the next week by pirogi, which I told them were Polish ravioli. That was A-OK with Desolina. For dessert I bought Häagen-Dazs ice cream bars. I beamed as I watched their faces light up in ecstasy they reserved for babies. The ice cream was rich and the Belgian chocolate sweet and bitter.

"*Dove hai comperato questa roba?*" Desolina asked. "Where did you buy these?"

"At C-Town Supermarket," I said. It was the store where they did their marketing.

"*Ma,* c'mon," she said, annoyedly.

"*E vero,*" I said. "It's true. I got them where they sell the ice cream."

She still didn't believe me, but it said a lot about how circumscribed their lives were. Hundreds of new products were being introduced to American consumers every year—haute cuisine TV dinners, blue corn tortilla chips, and Reeses Pieces breakfast cereal—but Tony and Desolina were oblivious. They pushed their cart down the same old aisles, for the same old pasta, milk, cannellini beans, tuna, Italian bread, apples, and bananas.

My grandparents were eating people. The thing they liked best about America was that you ate well not just on holidays, as they had done in Italy, but 365 days a year. That's what an American paycheck did. And now, in their early 90s, they were on a culinary adventure.

I pulled out all the stops: meatloaf dinners from a local diner, Chicken from the Colonel, New York Cheesecake, Campbell's Hearty soups, Ben & Jerry's Chubby Hubby.

The only failure was Chinese food. They ate it and didn't like it, I believe because they couldn't tell what was in it. Desolina kept asking me what the hell we were eating.

Perhaps the *piece de resistance* was when I appeared with McDonald's Quarter Pounders, fries, shakes, and apple pies. This was when the larger hamburgers were still packed in Styrofoam boxes. I put one in front of my grandmother, along with her fries and shake.

The fries she recognized. The shake, I pointed out, was *"latte e gelato,* milk and ice cream." She looked at the Styrofoam container, befuddled. I reached across the table and thumped the lid with my finger. The top popped open, revealing a large, steaming hamburger.

"Eeeeey!" she said with glee. "*Guarda, Tony, guarda!*"

Everything was a hit except the shakes. They could not understand why anyone would mix milk and ice cream.

Onward we marched: turkey and stuffing, western omelets, ice cream sandwiches. They were like children in a candy store. It got to the point that they began requesting these new foods, especially pizza. They would ask me for it sheepishly, as if it was something their mothers would have forbidden. I always obliged.

One winter day my wife, Gina, and I had gone to a museum that was a few blocks from my grandparents' building. It was six and dark when we left. I suggested we pay them an impromptu visit. So they would not feel they had to feed us, we brought along a large pizza.

We arrived in front of their building at a little before seven. Desolina's bedroom faced the street, and the light was out. When my wife pointed it out, I shrugged it off, saying they were in the main room watching Glen Campbell re-runs or pro basketball.

We climbed up the stoop, stepped into the vestibule, and rang the bell.

No answer.

I rang again.

No answer.

Gina said, "They're asleep."

I looked at my watch. "At 6:55? I don't think so."

I rang the bell again. "They're both a little deaf," I said.

No answer.

I gave the bell a final jab. Another. No one came.

"Ok, let's go," I said.

Tony and Desolina, who had grown up in a peasant farming village, were still creatures of that era: up at sunrise, abed at sunset.

As we turned to leave, my grandfather, dressed in his threadbare pajamas, appeared down the hallway and peered at us through the vestibule door, which was trimmed with see-through lace curtains. I parted the curtains. Afraid he would be angry at having been awakened, I waved hesitantly at him.

He couldn't have been more pleased. He opened the door and welcomed us in. While he was embracing Gina, I slipped into the apartment. Pizza grease was running down my wrist.

As I put down the pie on the table, Desolina came out of the bedroom. She was dressed in an old pink bathrobe. Her sleeping kerchief was askew. It had slipped down over one eye, making her look like a pirate. She was fumbling with her cat-eye glasses and squinting at me. As yet she had no idea who I was.

After she slipped them on and focused, she shouted, "No, no, go home! Too late! Nonna sleeping! Go home!"

"But, but . . ." I stammered.

"No, please, Jimmy, I'm tired. Go!"

She began shooing me out.

By this time, Gina and Tony had come in.

"Too late, Jimmy!" Desolina continued. "Everybody sleep now. See you next week. Bye-bye! Go home!"

I pointed to the table and said, "I brought pizza."

She looked down at the box, threw her arms open to me, and said, "Okay, come on in! Everybody sit down and eat. Tony, go to the kitchen to get some plates. Nice, very nice. C'mon, sit down, everybody, *mangiamo*. Jimmy, you want a beer?"

THE SANFORD DINER

As my grandparents aged, my father flew in from Michigan to see them on a regular basis. His visits always included lunch at the Sanford Restaurant on Astoria's Broadway, and I often went along. Because it was two blocks from their home, the event was an opportunity to get them a little exercise. They also liked the comfortable booths and glitzy chandeliers. The owner took a liking to them. He usually sent over complimentary glasses of the house white, which Desolina moved behind the catsup bottle and sugar packets, out of Tony's reach.

"*Dai* Desolina, what am I, a baby?!" he'd say, and she'd dutifully pass the wine to him.

Ordering wasn't easy because they did not read English well and we had to avoid a myriad of foods and ingredients that gave them digestive trouble. Rich dishes, which shot through their aged systems, could spell disaster on the stroll home.

When the menus came, Desolina said, "Everybody the same," because she wanted us to eat identical meals.

"Mama, how about some chicken today, with green beans and potatoes and some lentil soup?" my father asked.

"*Va bene,*" she replied. "That's fine. But what's Papa having?"

The menu had a dizzying array of choices, many in small print, so Tony deferred to my father.

"Pa, what do you feel like today? How about veal?"

"*Vitello,*" he replied. "Very good."

"How about with a baked potato e *carote*?"

"Very good," Tony replied.

"Selvi, what's Papa eating?" Desolina asked again.

"He's having veal."

"Ask him if he wants chicken instead," Desolina said.

15

"Mama, if you want chicken, have chicken!" my father scolded. "Why do you always have to have the same thing as Papa?"

"Because his food might be better than mine," she replied.

My father ordered her chicken, asking that it be prepared as blandly as possible: skin removed, easy on the salt, and no butter on the vegetables.

A busboy brought a basket of regular and sourdough rolls and breadsticks with sesame seeds, which they raided. After it was empty, my grandmother pushed it away and began looking towards the kitchen window for the arrival of her meal.

They ate heartily and wasted nothing, with Desolina spearing several leftover French fries off my plate, as you would expect from a woman raised on a daily fare of a corn mush called polenta.

Then came time for dessert.

"*Vuoi un dolce?*" I asked my grandmother. "Do you want dessert?

"I don't know. Is Papa having dessert?"

I leaned over to my grand father. "*Nonno, un dolce?*"

Tony thought for a moment. "*Sì.*"

"What do you want?" I asked. "How about pie? Fresh apple pie."

"Very good."

I turned to my grandmother. "He's having apple pie."

"Then I want pie, too," she said.

"O.K. Two apple pies."

"Jimmy, does Papa want it a la mode?" Desolina asked.

"*What?*"

"Does Papa want the pie a la mode? Ask him."

"Nonno, do you want your pie a la mode?"

"*Sì.*"

"Yes, he wants it a la mode."

"Good," replied Desolina. "Then I'll have mine a la mode, too."

THE VISITS

Within three years of marrying, Gina and I had two children, and they, too, became part of the Saturday ritual, which required lots more logistical planning than in my bachelor days.

We packed the stroller, the Snuggly, the diapers, the bottles, all of it. We hauled ourselves to the subway, changed at Times Square to the N train and got off at Broadway. We walked a few blocks and rang their buzzer. Desolina and Tony opened the door, and we burst in. Luca was released from the Snuggly, though not before Desolina kissed his feet. Alma was led by Tony to the kitchen, where he plied her with cookies. After having his diaper changed, Luca raced to the kitchen to get a sweet, too. Desolina followed the children around as if they were puppies unleashed in her apartment. They went into her bedroom to look at the tall bed and smell the mothballs coming from the closet. Desolina corralled them and said, "Gimme kiss," and they complied, though not on her right cheek, where she had a large mole. I got the children settled in front of the TV and began preparing lunch, though not before my grandmother had me spend two minutes adjusting her bedroom shade just so, because she was convinced neighbors were spying on her. The antipasti and breadsticks were brought out while the ravioli cooked. When they appeared, Gina cut them into eighths for the children. Of course, we ate in silence. Desolina used her breadstick like a croupier, shoving the serving dish of ravioli at anyone whose plate was empty, or using it to hook the container of Parmesan cheese and bring it to herself. When Alma left the table to go to the bathroom, Desolina thought she was done and cleaned her plate.

After lunch, we went outside, where the children walked up and down the arms of the stoop and ate ice cream from a deli down the block. Desolina applauded them from her chair. We returned inside. My grandparents were ready to eat again, but I held them off with a round of cards while the children kicked plastic fruit around the apartment. Then, supper: We had canned lentil soup and a platter of cheese and fruit. Alma ended up with a lentil on her cheek that made her look like Desolina. The air in the apartment was stale and soporific. Summer, winter, or fall, my grandparents rarely opened their windows. Gina drank Nescafe to keep herself awake. She caught my eye and nodded towards the door. Finally, I said the word that broke their heart: *"andiamo,"* "we're going." Desolina looked as if we were sailing off to some strange country to seek our fortune, as she had done sixty years earlier.

"Prossima settimana," she asked, "next week?"

"Sì," I replied, even though I didn't know if I'd bring the children. The trip was too exhausting. It would be two weeks, probably three, when I again shepherded the entire family over, but no matter how frequently we came, when we arrived, they acted as if we had been away one hundred years.

BUON COMPLEANNO

Tony and Desolina did not celebrate their birthdays. It was not done in the old country, they told me. But this was America.

I began celebrating their birthdays when I moved to New York. in 1983. They were surprised when I showed up one afternoon in July with an ice cream cake, and candles to celebrate Tony's big day. There were no presents. He was impossible to buy for.

"*Buon compleanno*," I said. "Happy birthday."

Tony got a kick out of blowing out the candles, and he had two slices of cake, one less than Desolina.

With the children, the parties became more elaborate. Gina always made sure we brought a gift, even if it was a kerchief from a 5 & Dime. There were party hats, horns, up-ups, and festive napkins. Desolina loved the preparation and directed me as to the placement of balloons that were taped to light fixtures, picture frames, and door knobs.

Tony would not wear a conical party hat (no one who'd ever adorned his head with a Bersagliere hat could stoop that low), but he blew the horn a few times, for the pleasure of his grandchildren.

The sweets varied: Chocolate cake, Howard Johnson's coconut cake, and once, a Carvel ice cream cake, which my grandmother complained about because she was being cheated out of real cake.

By far, her favorite was apple pie. I poked as many candles into the crust as I could without undermining its structure and brought the pie in under dimmed lights. We sang. Her hat cocked at a 45-degree angle, Desolina blew her horn at the children. As I cut the pie, a hunk of crust fell off. Her hand scuttled across the table, snatched it, and brought it to her mouth. The children laughed.

I asked Desolina, "*Cuanti anni hai*? How old are you?"

"*Ottanta!*" she said. "Eighty!"

This was a running joke. She always took ten years off.

"*Non e vero,*" I said. "That's not true."

"All right, *sono settanta,*" she said, "I'm seventy."

"I don't believe it," I said.

"*Guarda qui,*" she said, holding out her hands.

She was right: Her skin was as supple and smooth and creamy as the vanilla ice cream that melted slowly atop her pie.

GOOD BEER

After Tony retired in 1966, his doctor made him give up cigars and whiskey. All he had left was beer. He consumed only two cans a day. At around 11 a.m., he got his Schlitz from under the kitchen sink and guzzled them one after the other, I guess because it generated a light buzz.

This was fine for a long time, but eventually we noticed that Tony was getting a little wobbly on his feet. My father was worried he'd fall and break a hip.

We put our heads together. We had to find a solution because beer was one of Tony's last pleasures left in his life. We decided to try non-alcoholic beer. I went down to the C-Town supermarket and came back with two six packs of Moussy, a non-alcoholic brew made in Switzerland. I put them under the sink and said nothing.

When my father came to visit several days later, he rushed to the sink to see if the ersatz beer had been consumed. Had Tony discovered the switch, he would have raised hell. My father let out a sigh of relief when he saw a six-pack gone. He went down to C-Town to do the week's marketing and returned with a case of Moussy.

As he unloaded the groceries, Tony shuffled into the kitchen for his 11 a.m. beer. He took two cans and set them on the counter. He pried open the tops with a butter knife. With a hand on his hip, he took a long slug. He pulled the can away from his face and studied it. My father, shelving pasta and olive oil, watched him nervously out of the corner of his eye. Tony finished the beer and studied the can again. He crushed and dropped it in a garbage bag.

He picked up the second can and pondered. My father's heart was pounding. He was sure the jig was up. Tony was going to call his bluff.

Tony drank again. He turned to my father and said, in English, "Son, this beer's no fucking good."

"Well, Papa, I . . ."

"What has happened to beer in this country?!" Tony continued. "We used to have such good beer, now it's nothing but junk! The Germans know how to make beer! Where have the Germans gone? The best beer I ever had was in Austria, when I was a soldier in 1918. It was a hot day and that beer went down . . ."

The spiel went on for a few minutes. Finally, Tony tossed back the second can and said, with resignation, "Well, whatya gonna do?"

He shrugged and shuffled out.

STATI UNITI

United States

Tony's first American passport

FIRST DAY ON THE JOB

In 1953, my father applied for his first job in the sales division of the Upjohn pharmaceutical company. A part of the application process included interviews with family members. My mother, engaged to my father at the time, was pulled out of class by a nun at the College of Mount St. Vincent and led to a small room, where two men from the company were waiting to talk to her. After friendly banter, the men began asking serious questions, most of which focused on whether she would willingly accompany her husband if he got transferred to a different part of the country. Yes, of course I will, she answered, again and again. The men seemed pleased and went away.

The other interviewees, much to my father's chagrin, were his parents. Their English was poor. He wondered how long the interviewers could converse with Tony and Desolina before everyone ran out of things to say.

My father was even a little worried about the neighborhood. (This was before my grandparents moved to Astoria in the late 1950s.). Hell's Kitchen was a tough Irish-Italian neighborhood, especially if you were an outsider. Located on Manhattan's middle west side, the area was a combination of tenements, rail yards, and warehouses. On summer nights, when the wind was blowing from the west, my father would lie in bed and listen to the lowing of cattle and the baaing of sheep in a nearby slaughterhouse. The peace was shattered when the animals, smelling the blood of their brethren a few paces ahead, began to wail and scream. If the wind was strong enough, the smell of blood wafted into my father's window.

Nevertheless, a day was appointed. The two men, Max and Val, were to come at 7:30 p.m. My father left word with the thugs on the block that Max's Ford was not to be meddled with.

After huffing up four flights of stairs to the apartment, Val and Max got a warm welcome from Tony and Desolina. Everyone took a seat at the kitchen table and made small talk. My grandfather was pretty good at this, while Desolina nodded and smiled. Soon it became evident that refreshments were in order. My grandfather offered his guests whiskey or bourbon. There was also beer, purchased by my father because he knew Max loved cold beer. Max could have been at the finest restaurant in France, but would have ordered a Rheingold on draft.

Tony also offered wine, homemade, he noted, if they would like to try some. Probably to be polite, the two men signaled wine as their choice, and Tony dispatched my father down to the cellar, where each tenant had a small storage space. In addition to wine, my grandparents used it to store cheese and salami. My father unlocked the door—whose lower half was covered with tin so rats couldn't gnaw their way through the wood—fetched a bottle, and returned to the apartment.

By this time, Desolina had served cake, and Tony was waxing philosophic about America's greatness. Here, there were opportunities for the working man to eat well and send his children to decent schools. My father uncorked and poured the wine. Max and Val raised their glasses and drank. The wine went down smoothly, unexpectedly so for Max. He soon emptied his glass and asked for another.

Tony talked on and on. Max relayed his thoughts about the greatness of America—for example, the fact that in a single generation, a man like Tony, with a fourth-grade education, could send a son to college. Val concurred with everything that had been said. Desolina said nothing, just bade her guests to eat. More wine was consumed. It was time for another bottle.

Tony motioned to his son to go down to the cellar. This time, to save himself an extra trip, if necessary, my father came up with two bottles. They were actually empty champagne bottles, which my grandfather got from a friend in the restaurant business, and so a bit larger than average wine bottles. This time, Tony himself took the corkscrew to do the honors. While the screw was penetrating the cork he bragged a little about how his wine was made with only the finest grapes. Max wasn't as interested in the provenance of the grape as he was in getting his glass refilled. This was the best damn wine he had ever tasted, he said. He would think twice now about automatically ordering beer.

Down the wine went. More cake and cookies were eaten. The other bottle was opened. Everyone was loosening up. It didn't matter anymore that Tony's English wasn't so good or that he kept repeating himself. Or that Max was slurring a little. Everyone understood what everyone else was trying to say.

My father's drinking did not keep pace with that of his guests. He had to keep a level head; he was engaged to be married. This job meant good money. Max's face was getting flushed. He was very happy.

When the third bottle went dry, Tony stated, "I make white wine, too."

"White?!" asked Max, excitedly.

"Would you like to try some?"

Max and Val said, "Sure!"

Tony jerked his thumb towards the door. My father got up with a sense of foreboding: Not only did mixing red and white cause hangovers, but his father had shouted *"Porta su du boti!"* ("Bring up two bottles!") as he headed out the door.

Max enjoyed the white nearly as much as the red. Tony showed him how Italians dunked their cake in wine. They continued to talk, the men smoking cigarettes, Tony puffing away on a Toscano cigar.

After three hours, the evening was over. Everyone felt that it was a success. Val and my father helped Max down the stairs and packed him into the car. Val was sober enough to drive Max home.

The next afternoon, my father got a call from Val to tell him he had gotten the job. It was really Max's place to call, since he had seniority, but he was at home with a monstrous hangover, Val said.

Tony was very pleased when the news was delivered that evening. All the sacrifice he had made by coming over to America, the long hours he worked, the saving and scrimping, it had paid off.

"And how much will be you making?" he asked my father.

"Four thousand dollars a year," my father said.

Tony looked up at the ceiling to give thanks to the heavens. He had been a working stiff for forty years and didn't make close to that kind of dough.

"And a company car, too," my father added.

"*Una macchina!*" my grandfather said with pure pleasure. "A car!" He and Desolina didn't even know how to drive.

My father was not slated to begin the job until after the New Year. He reported to work after the holidays and was told to go to the personnel office to fill out some paperwork. He was informed that, like all employees of the company, he would be receiving an automatic cost-of-living salary increase of four percent.

That evening, at dinner, my grandfather asked his son how his first day of work went. There was not too much my father could explain to his parents about selling pharmaceuticals, so he went into little detail. As for cost-of-living increase—well, how could you ever explain that concept to peasants? So, my father simply said, "By the way, Pa, I'm not making $4,000. My salary was increased to $4,160."

Tony just about gagged on his gnocchi. He looked over at his wife, pounded the table, and said, "Can you believe it Desolina? One day on the job, and he gets a $160 raise! What a job! What a company! God bless America!"

CITIZENSHIP

Desolina did not bother to apply for U.S. citizenship because she believed she would return to Italy after my grandfather had made his fortune. However, during World War II, Italian aliens in New York had to report regularly to an immigration government office so their movements could be watched, and Desolina grew tired of this routine. Moreover, it didn't look like she would be returning to Italy to live high on the hog anytime soon—not with Tony making $45 per week. She decided it was time to become a U.S. citizen.

She dispatched my father down to the immigration office to get an application. Among the papers he brought back was a booklet with sample questions that might be asked during the exam. Desolina's English was poor because she rarely ventured out of the neighborhood and, in her interactions with the outside world, she was assisted by family and friends. Now she would have to stand before an examiner alone.

My father tried to get her to study, but she didn't take it seriously.

"Who makes the laws of the United States government?" he asked, sitting at the kitchen table while she cooked.

"*Ai-bo!* Ugh! What do you mean who makes the laws? The politicians make the laws, and they make them in their own self-interest," Desolina said.

"How many years does a U.S. Supreme Court Justice serve?"

"Too many," she said, throwing breadcrumbs in a mixing bowl. "*Ai-bo!*"

My father shook his head; Tony smirked behind his newspaper.

On the big day, my father accompanied his mother to the exam. He stood next to her as the examiner began the questions.

"Who freed the slaves?" he asked.

29

Desolina looked over at my father and asked, "*Cos la dit?* What did he say?"

My father responded to her in Italian, "He wants to know who freed the . . ."

"Hey! Hey! Who are you?!" yelled the examiner, pointing an accusing finger at my father.

"I'm her son," he replied. "She doesn't understand English very well, so I thought I would translate . . ."

"You'll keep your mouth shut," said the man. "I am the one who asks questions here. Understood?"

My father nodded.

The examiner had an Italian name, though it was clear from his diction and demeanor that neither he nor his parents were just off the boat.

He shuffled some papers. He spoke in broken Italian: "Signora Vescovi, today I ask you question so you become American citizen, OK?"

Desolina nodded obediently.

"*Allora, e vero che Abraham Lincoln ha liberato I schiavi?*" ("Is it true that Abraham Lincoln freed the slaves?")

Desolina hesitated, then said, "Yes."

"*Brava!*" said the judge. "*Brava, Signora Vescovi. Allora, numero due: E vero che George Washington era il primo presidente degli Stati Uniti?*"

"Yes," said Desolina, now with a dash more confidence.

"*Molto bene, Signora!*" said the judge. "*Numero tre: E anche vero, Signora, che un senatore sta in uffocio per sei anni?* "(Is it also true that a senator's term in office is six years?")

"*Ma si!*" said my grandmother, "but of course!"

And so Desolina passed with flying colors.

On the day she, with a few hundred other newly-minted U.S. citizens, took the oath of allegiance she was again accompanied by my father. A judge asked the candidates to raise their right hand and then, in English spiced by a dozen accents, the crowd took the oath more or less in unison.

My father was watching his mother. It was clear she didn't know any of the words. She moved her mouth up and down, like a Charlie McCarthy doll. Half way through, she turned around to him and winked.

THE TELEPHONE

Even three weeks after my grandparents had gotten a telephone in 1954, when someone called, Desolina would stand over my grandfather's shoulder asking, "*Chi è morto? Tutti all right?* Did someone die? Is everyone all right?" The telephone was a precious device for my grandmother, one to be respected and used sparingly. Until her dying day in 1997, the phone was never a convenience. In her mind it was a tool used for emergencies and to communicate important bits of information, which included the weather. The quicker you returned the receiver to its cradle the better.

Given her feelings about the phone, Desolina approached answering machines with untoward suspicion when they became commonplace in the 1980s. In the end, I faced with her the same problem my father had struggled with his entire life: how to explain to his parents the workings of a custom, an economic principle, or a device of the 20th century.

In the end, I decided I wasn't going to even try. After all, the first time Desolina saw a tape recorder—I had brought one over to play Italian hill songs from a tape a friend in Milan had sent me—she clasped her hands together and said, "Just like a Victrola!" What words could I string together to illustrate that even though the voice on the machine was mine, I was not at home, that she should not say anything until she heard a BEEP, and that she should then leave her name and number and a brief message?

The outcome of this was that on more than one occasion I arrived home to hear her voice on the tape yelling "*bastardo!*" or "son-na-ma-bitch!" She had obviously called, gotten the machine, and heard that voice yak on without interruption. Then she got a loud BEEP in her ear, followed by dead silence, as if she had been hung up on. Had I received that treatment, I would have yelled "bastard!" too.

One afternoon I brought my roommate, Steve, for lunch at my grandparents' apartment. I liked doing this because it broke up a routine that could be pretty monotonous—shopping, eating, stoop sitting, Briscola. Tony and Desolina relished having visitors. Any friend of mine was a friend of theirs. Besides, guests always gave my grandmother a chance to size up my eating. If the guest out-ate me, she would harangue me during my next visit about how Steve or Bill or Frank were good boys because the cleaned their plates and took third helpings. Well, of course they did this; they were being polite. I, on the other hand, had to pace myself for weekly feeds.

Steve was a hit. He was good-looking and friendly, and two minutes after arriving at their apartment he'd sized up the situation. Eat first, talk later, even if there isn't much to talk about, and expect to be hugged by Desolina once or twice during your visit. Steve really ascended in her eyes when we played a card game called Briscola. He caught on fast and turned out to be a skillful—if not a little ruthless—player, which Desolina, his partner, savored. She later told me that "this boy" was welcome to come back "anytime."

Her view of Steve changed radically a few weeks later. After I walked into their apartment, Desolina asked me, "Who is this boy you live with?" What she meant was "What kind of a man is this that you would reside under the same roof as he?"

I knew something was wrong, but before I could get to the bottom of it, she said, "He's fresh, this boy! No good!"

She went on to explain how she tried to call me, but that he answered and he went on talking ("Blah, blah, blah!" she said) and then he beeped her ear and hung up. In fact, he did it twice before she gave up.

"He did this for spite!" she said. "After I gave him a nice meal, extra cake, we played cards, watched TV together." She shook her head in disbelief at his ingratitude. "For spite!"

To come to Steve's defense, I finally had to face the moment I'd been avoiding: explain an answering machine.

I began with the tape recorder I had once brought over to play Italian music. This machine, I said, was the same, except it was connected to a phone and allowed people to let their party know they had called. My explanation went on and on, probably for too long.

My grandfather also listened in. He seemed to understand the concept, but was skeptical that I would have such a machine. It sounded too complex, too important. Maybe Mayor Koch or President Reagan had one, but not me.

As for Desolina, she was convinced that I was telling a wild, sci-fi story to make excuses for Steve. She would have none of it, and for the rest of her days referred to Steve as "bastard man" or "the fresh one."

"IL WRESTLING"

One thing my siblings and I loved about coming to New York was that Tony and Desolina got so many TV channels. Long before the days of cable, their set could pick up twelve, which in our eyes, was a boon.

In Astoria, we saw "Abbot & Costello" and countless cartoons, westerns, and detective shows. Tony and Desolina let us eat biscotti and watch until our eyes grew bleary.

There was only one rule: My grandparents got control of the set when wrestling came on. Watching them watch wrestling was a source of fascination for my siblings and me. They believed every punch, every face smash, every time someone was heaved out of the ring, was real. They sat on the edge of the couch and pounded the arms and howled when their man, usually an Italian, got slammed around the ring. Sometimes the opponent had a weapon, such as a roll of pennies, which everyone in the arena knew about except for the referee. Bam! Down to the mat went their beloved Bruno San Martino! While he was trying to get up, his opponent would stick him with a safety pin.

"Guarda! Guarda! Cretino!" Desolina yelled at the ref. "Look! Look you idiot!"

"Porco cane!" Tony would holler.

There was rage in his eyes. He clenched his fist and looked up at the heavens, as if to ask God, "Why don't you help him, you lazy bum?!"

My siblings and I had seen plenty of Three Stooges episodes to know good slapstick when we saw it. We tried to assure our grandparents that the kicking and pricking and head-stomping weren't real.

"Look, that guy's fist isn't touching Bruno's face!" my brother would say. Or, "That's too thick for blood, Nonna—it's catsup!"

Desolina waved us off and turned back to the match, just as her man went flying out of the ring.

"Aiuto!" she cried. "Help!"

One evening my father came in during a match. Desolina and Tony were bound up in knots; their wrestler was getting strangled in the ropes.

"Dad!" we cried. "Tell them—tell them in Italian—it's not real!"

My father rolled his eyes and replied, "I've been trying for twenty years. Forget it."

POM-POMS

Desolina made pom-poms. New York's garment district was a block away from Hell's Kitchen, and she would walk over to a shop on the fourth floor of a nondescript building, get wool or silk, and come back to the house, where she worked at a special table Tony had built for her. The table had two pegs in the front corners. Desolina wrapped the yarn from peg to peg and held it there with clothespins. With a piece of string, she tied the yarn very tightly at regular intervals, tying off each section as one does to make sausage. She cut each section in the middle of the adjacent strings, and with a steel comb, brushed and teased the wool into the shape of a ball. She made a thousand pom-poms per week, which brought in about $20, half of Tony's salary. There were big pom-poms for hats, and little ones for curtains, slippers, and shawls.

These pom-poms served an additional purpose late one Christmas Eve when Anna Lanza from down the hall showed up at their apartment with a tree that was being discarded by a man who'd been selling them on Ninth Avenue. Desolina, who answered Anna's knock, didn't know what to do with the small, scrawny pine. She and my grandfather had never bought one, and they had nothing with which to decorate it.

Desolina brought it inside just as my grandfather came out from his bedroom.

"*Un albero di Natale*," Desolina said. "A Christmas tree." She shrugged.

"Now we have to decorate it," he said.

She threw her hands up, as if to say, "With what?"

My father pointed to the pom-pom table, where his mother's materials lay.

She shrugged, as if to say, "Why not?'

36

Desolina sat down. She was very fast. In no time she had made two dozen pom-poms—red, blue, yellow, and white that my father and grandfather hung on the tree with small loops from the string. They sat around the tree and waited until midnight, when they bid each other a *"Buon Natale."*

APPLIANCES

My grandparents were the last among their friends to buy appliances. They were positively awed by, but uneasy about these shiny, humming objects such as refrigerators, ranges, mixing bowls, percolators, and the like. Their philosophy was, "Why change things when life was running smoothly?"

Ultimately, however, they could not resist the temptation of convenience. With a refrigerator instead of an icebox, they would not have to rush home from someone's house because they had forgotten to empty the drip pan before leaving.

They bought a refrigerator in 1946 at Macy's. My father accompanied them to make sure they understood all the salesman had to say. Four days later, the unit, a Westinghouse Shelvador, arrived. It was white with a cobalt blue handle. Desolina got upset because she didn't know where to put it. It could not fit where the icebox had been, and she didn't want it blocking the window because it would be bad for her eyes while making pom poms.

They tried the Shelvador in several places, including next to the bath tub (which was in the kitchen), but that seemed unhealthy. Finally, they moved it where the table was, and put the table under the window.

There was a similar problem when they bought a TV in 1953. There was no space for it in the kitchen, the social room of the house. My father's room was not nearly big enough to accommodate the three of them for a wrestling broadcast; it was hardly bigger than a closet. It finally went in my grandparents' bedroom. The awkward location meant that they didn't use the set often, though this wasn't a great tragedy. They didn't understand Milton Berle or care for the evening news. They watched "The Glen Campbell Show," the Macy's Thanksgiving Day Parade, and wrestling.

These modern conveniences were paid for in cash. My grandmother looked suspiciously on the notion of credit. "*Si deve fare il passo come si ha lungo la gamba,*" she said. "The step you take should only be as long as your leg."

Before the telephone arrived, all calls had to be made at the Alps Drugstore on Ninth Avenue. It went in Tony and Desolina's bedroom. The word went out to all their friends that no calls were received after 8:30 p.m. because Tony was in bed. He rose very early to get to his terrazzo jobs, which were sometimes located in New Jersey and Long Island. (Terrazzo is a type of flooring made of cement mixed with chips of marble or granite and ground to a high finish.)

When someone rang after that hour, he would explode from the bedroom, "*Porco cane! Ma, chi chiama a questa'ora?!* Who could be calling at this hour?!"

When Desolina used the phone, I couldn't help but think of the child of an astronaut who, at Houston Control, had been allowed to talk to her daddy, but only for a few seconds. One April, with tax deadline looming, she asked me to prepare her 1040 form because she no longer wanted to pay a neighbor lady to do it. After all, here was a grandson with a college education. Why couldn't he do them? I had two young children at home and didn't have the time or energy and made up some excuse.

So, she called my brother, Mark (yet another college grad). He lived in Canada— Vancouver to be exact. To Desolina, Canada was a country just above America. She didn't realize how far west it went. She rang my brother at 8 a.m. For him it was 5 a.m.

"Hello, Marco? Marco, it's Nonna!"

He thought it might be an emergency.

"Nonna, is everything all right?"

"Yeah, yeah, *tutti* all right. Marco, listen, can you do my tax?"

Still half asleep, he replied, "I can't, Nonna. I live in Canada."

"O.K. Bye-bye," she said, and she hung up.

THE WORLD'S FAIR

My grandparents took my father to the 1939 New York World's Fair. Tony was anxious to see the fair, having laid terrazzo in a number of its buildings. Desolina was anxious to visit because, as a young girl, she had heard about the great European fairs in Paris and other cities.

They took the subway out to Flushing, Queens, and spent the entire day touring the World of Tomorrow, the Lagoon of Nations, and other magnificent halls. Desolina even let my father go on the bumper cars. For lunch, they ate hot dogs and got milkshakes from the Borden's Pavilion and free gum from Wrigley's. It was one of the few times my grandparents spent the day out (except at the home of a friend) and did not bring their own food.

By late afternoon, Desolina's feet were a wreck. On the way to the subway, still at the fair grounds, she had to sit down every few minutes, remove her shoes, and rub her aching soles. Finally, she spotted a machine onto which you stepped and into which you dropped a penny to make foot pedals vibrate. She got on line. When it was her turn, she climbed onto the contraption and dropped a coin into the slot. The pedals, shaped like feet, oscillated, and she let out a sigh of relief loud enough to be heard on the tip of Long Island.

"*O, che miracolo!*" she said. "What a miracle!"

When the machine stopped, she carefully got off and went to the rear of the line.

"Tony, *da me ancora un centesim,*" she said. "Give me another penny."

NO CHARGE FOR THE LABOR

Every few years, Tony and Desolina would board a train and come see us in Kalamazoo. Tony mostly spent his days puttering around in the yard. He rebuilt a patio, re-planed the garden soil and made sure the lawn was watered. He used to stare at the sprinkler and nod in appreciation.

He also spent a day touring the Upjohn plant, which had miles and miles of assembly lines where millions of pills dropped into bottles. He had lunch in the executive dining room.

On the way out, he and my father crossed paths with the CEO. My father introduced him as "*il padrone delle compagnia*, the boss of the company."

When the CEO asked Tony how he liked the Upjohn facilities, my grandfather said, in broken English, that he was very impressed. This was why America was a great nation, such machinery, such productivity, and all making medicine for people around the world. In his day, he had to walk eight miles to see a doctor, who often didn't have medicine. No, this place was truly great.

But, what was not so great, Tony continued, was the terrazzo in the lobby. The craftsmanship was awful, my grandfather continued. It was a disgrace to the trade and such a great company deserved better.

However, since he was so grateful that Upjohn had given his son a wonderful position, enabling him to afford a beautiful home, two cars, and admission in a fancy country club, he himself would return with his tools in a year, after his official retirement, and lead a crew to re-do the entire floor, at no charge. Of course, Upjohn would have to pay for the materials, but, he repeated, for the labor, there would be no charge.

EXTRA COLLEGE

After I arrived in New York to earn an M.A. in English at Columbia University, my grandmother took me aside and said, "I thought you finished college. What are you really doing in New York?" So, yet again, I had to find a way to explain to them a very foreign idea.

What exactly was 'graduate school'? they wanted to know. They had always thought that college was as high as a human could go.

"I want to be a professor, and to be a professor you have to go to . . . more . . . college," I bumbled.

My grandmother let that sink in and said, "You mean you went to college for four years and now you can go higher?"

"That's right," I replied.

My grandfather, who had just awakened from a nap on the couch, said, "God bless America! More college!"

"What more can you learn after college?" Desolina asked, skeptically.

I rolled my eyes. What was I going to tell her? That I was going to deconstruct Shakespeare's plays? Analyze T.S. Eliot's poetry?

"Desolina, what's the matter with you?!" my grandfather shouted. "Extra college! *Capito*? Extra college!"

Desolina always cowered when he snapped at her. She smiled at me and said approvingly "Oh, extra college. Nice . . ."

"God bless America!" my grandfather reiterated.

And so for that year of study my graduate work at Columbia University was always referred to as "extra college."

Tony and Desolina attended my commencement with great fanfare. It was a cool day in May. I waited for them outside Columbia's black gates at Broadway and 116th Street. My father had gone from his Midtown hotel out to Queens to pick them up. I soon spotted them emerging from a field of yellow cabs crammed in front of the gates.

I knew it was their taxi because it took so long for them to extricate themselves. As I approached, I heard my grandfather yelling, "*Porco cane, Desolina!* Are you going to look again?! We saw it three minutes ago. *E nella borsa*, it's in your purse! *Fa presto!* C'mon!"

He was referring to $1,000 that he and my grandmother were going to give me as a gift for getting through "extra college." It was in cash. They never had a checking account and used money orders when paying bills.

I walked my grandfather to the curb and went back for the others. My father was getting his mother out of the vehicle by rocking her back and forth.

"*Uno, due, tre!* One, two, three!"

He finally hauled her out and we hurried to the curb. While embraces were going round, Desolina took the opportunity to check her purse again.

I guided them onto campus to a row of empty wooden chairs on a cobble-stoned walkway, far away from the dais.

"Right here, this is good," said my father.

"Why not up closer?" I asked. "There are seats available."

He pointed to a restroom sign nearby. Referring to his parents, he said, "I've got to keep these people within striking distance, if you know what I mean."

I nodded. Then we heard a crash and a scream and looked over to see Desolina sprawled on the ground with a chair lying over her.

"*Cara!*" my grandfather yelled as he rushed to her aid. She was on the ground, crying. She had a scrape on her leg.

When Desolina had sat down, her chair leg had been driven into a space between cobblestones. The chair went off balance and down she went.

Columbia security guards came running over, asking if an ambulance was needed. My father sized up the situation. Desolina had had a number of operations in life. She did not handle pain well and she blubbered about the slightest hurt, but he knew she was a tough old bird.

"Mama, can you move your legs?" he asked.

She could. He had her sit up.

He sized her up again.

"Let's pull her to her feet," he told the guards.

They did, with hesitation, but up she went, clutching her purse. When she got to her feet, Desolina seemed pleasantly surprised to find she was in one solid piece. The crowd dispersed, though not before she thanked the people for their concern.

Relief crossed my father's face. He looked around for a chair, planted it firmly on the ground, and helped her sit. He did not scold her when she opened her purse to check again for the cash.

The ceremony began. The brass band struck up the Columbia anthem. Blue and white banners hanging from the McKim, Mead & White buildings rippled in the wind. The dais was filled with professors in their academic plumage. There were speeches. At one point during the proceedings, I looked back at my family. They were gone. I looked back again 10 minutes later. There they were. It had been a bathroom break.

Towards the end of the event, I turned around again. They were standing, my grandfather looking proudly on. He didn't really understand what this "extra college" was but he knew that I had gone a step further than even his son and this was what America was all about, and here we were in this impressive quad with these gorgeous buildings. Each one probably had enough terrazzo to fill a football field and if a building had terrazzo floors it was a place to be associated with.

My grandmother, meanwhile, was gazing up at my father with squinting eyes. She looked like a mole in the sunlight. My father was talking to her and wildly gesturing with his hands. As he talked, his movements got more emphatic. He looked annoyed. It was clear he wasn't getting through. She continued to peer at him with the mole look. Later, in a cab on the way to a restaurant, I asked him what he had been explaining to her. He rolled his eyes and said, "Extra college."

The site of the celebration meal was a restaurant on East 62nd Street called Il Vagabondo. In front was a long bar, behind that was a bocce alley, and upstairs was the restaurant. It was owned by some distant relatives of ours, on my mother's side. As we edged our way into the crowded place, my father was trying to catch the eye of the owner to see if we could get a little VIP treatment—namely, to be moved up to the front of the line. It had been a long day, and my father wanted to get his parents fed and home. They had insisted on eating out; no celebration was complete without a special meal. Finally, the owner recognized my father, and we got a table.

Menus arrived. My father chose for them, skipping dishes he thought might give them digestive trouble.

"*Pollo*, Ma, how about chicken? Some potatoes, green beans, all right?"

Desolina was at her most agreeable in restaurants. To have someone cook for you was a luxury.

"All right," she said, "but just ask the man to bring us more bread."

The basket was already empty. My father and I had had one buttered slice each; my grandparents had devoured the rest.

"*É 'l vino?*" asked Tony. "Where's the wine?"

My father ordered. Tony nodded with pleasure and grabbed his fork and knife, hoping the food would come within ten seconds.

A few minutes later, the waiter came with more bread and a bottle of wine, courtesy of the owner, who congratulated me, told me to say hello to my mother (his 3rd cousin, or something like that) and went off. My father was glaring at his mother. Despite his pleas, she insisted on wearing her hat. It was a woolen cap, like the kind longshoremen wear, blue knit and ratty looking. He kept telling her to take it off, but she refused, saying she was cold. My grandfather had kept his Fedora on, too. My father shrugged at me, as if to say, I hope you're not embarrassed. It was the first time in my life that I realized Desolina and Tony were still peasants, yokels from the sticks. To this day, it makes me proud.

My grandparents continued to devour the bread. One time we'd taken them to the Old Homestead, a fancy steakhouse in New York's meat district with huge portions. Tony and Desolina ordered mammoth prime rib dinners and, while waiting, kept digging into the basket of fresh-baked rolls. After bringing the third basket, the waiter leaned over to my father and said, "Sir, I don't know if your parents know this but there is *a lot* of food coming." My father looked up at him and said, "You don't know these people."

And, of course, they cleaned their plates at Il Vagabondo and had room left for espresso and cake.

On my next visit, Desolina, still confused by this "extra college" business, asked me what I was now going to do. My plans of going for a Ph.D. had been jettisoned. In no uncertain terms, my Columbia professors had let it be known that I was not doctoral timber. I had landed a job at a real estate trade magazine. I would be interviewing developers and writing stories about new condo and townhouse communities. Since that was too confusing to explain I simply said, *"journalista."* That was close enough, I thought.

Desolina looked at me with disbelief and said, "You think this is big thing?"

I had thought the profession would sound rather impressive to these peasants, but obviously I was mistaken.

I had to defend myself. "Well, but a *journalista* is a very important job . . . ."

She scoffed at that idea. She grunted, "Extra college and now you are going to be a *journalista*?"

It took about five minutes to realize that Desolina thought I was going to be one of the little men in the green newsstands that peddles newspapers, magazines, and Chicklets on 34th Street and Seventh Avenue.

No, I am going to write the stories, I explained. I got a copy of the local Italo-American paper, *Il Progresso*, and pointed to a by-line. My name will go here.

Desolina seemed satisfied, but not entirely.

BAPTISTS AND CHEESE

Some visitors who came to my grandparents' home understood them; others like Bill, a fervent Baptist, did not. As we ate, he tried to witness to my grandparents about his faith. While in no way exhibiting arrogance, he knew Tony and Desolina were Catholic and was genuinely concerned that their souls were not saved. He also talked at length about "what the Lord Jesus was doing" in his life.

Desolina responded, "Nice. Eat." She shoved the soup pot at him.

Bill kept it up through the fruit course and then dessert. He was probably the first protestant who ever dined at their home, and he was using bible tract phrases that to most Catholics, not to mention Italian peasants, must have sounded like a Sumerian: "making God the lord of my life" and "Jesus is the Alpha and Omega."

"Eat now, talk later," my grandmother said.

By the end of lunch, Bill had given up. Desolina produced a pack of cards, and we began playing Briscola. Bill didn't understand the game, but was a good sport when Desolina trounced him.

"They're good old folks, your grandparents," Bill said as we walked to the subway. "I'll be praying for them."

Perhaps the most exotic visitor to cross their threshold was Frank, a student from Taiwan whom I lived with during graduate school. He comprehended Tony and Desolina the moment he laid eyes on them.

They had never had an Asian guest in their home. Desolina wanted to make him feel welcome, so she spoke for twenty minutes about the "nice China people" who operated her green grocery. Except her grocer, like so many during the 1980s, were Korean (and themselves New York's latest immigrants). Frank took no offense. He looked over at me and winked.

And he took no offense when Desolina chided him for refusing to eat cheese ravioli. While Frank liked much Western culture and food, cheese, he told me, was nothing short of disgusting to him and most Chinese, who viewed it as sour, semi-hardened milk. He wouldn't touch it, any more than I think Desolina would've eaten sea cucumber had she been at Frank's house.

Still, my grandmother kept shaking her head at his refusal. She finally put a few on a plate and sent it down to him.

"Eat," she insisted, "eat."

"No, thank you, thank you very-very much," he said.

She said to me, "*Credo che é malato, questo uomo–non mangia niente.* I think this man is sick, he doesn't eat anything."

She turned back to Frank. "Eat!"

"Thank you very much."

He thanked her again and kept bowing from his end of the able until she finally gave up.

BROOKS BROTHERS

During his summers between college, my father worked as a longshoreman, a New York Public Library page, and a stock boy at Brooks Brothers. Every summer the store held its annual employees sale, a chance to get top-quality clothing at rock-bottom prices: shirts $.50, suits $20.

He bought a woolen suit for his father, who immediately fell in love with it. They brought it to a neighborhood tailor, but he wanted too much to take it down three sizes.

"I don't trust a bum like him with that beautiful suit, anyway," Tony muttered as they left the shop.

At work the next day, my father approached the head tailor who, in some ways, was the most important employee in the store. If word got around that he was poor at his trade, suits wouldn't sell. My father explained the situation, making sure to emphasize that Tony was "an immigrant just like you. He's never owned a suit like this. It would be a real honor for him."

"Bring him down here Saturday morning at 8 a.m.," the tailor said, without looking up from his stitching. Tony showed up in the suit and soon it was covered with enough chalk marks to make it look pin stripped.

"Give me a month," said the tailor.

When my father picked it up, he was told there would be no charge for the alterations.

The suit fit like a glove, and Tony wore the garment at every opportunity: funerals, dances, and dinners. The last time he put it on was at my wedding in 1987. It wasn't in respectable enough shape for him to be buried in it six years later. Instead, he was laid to rest in a Barney's suit he'd bought before the store became *chic*—in the era when they still gave you two pair of slacks with the jacket and no charge for the cuffs.

LOST IN TRANSLATION

As he rose in rank, my father had an increasingly difficult time explaining to his parents what he did. "Salesman" was easy, "product manager" was somewhat difficult but doable, "director of marketing" was hard, and "general manager of Upjohn international" was nearly impossible. They looked at him as if he was talking about the Theory of Relativity.

Still, my father never gave up. It wasn't so much that he wanted to toot his own horn. Rather, he desired to make them aware that their sacrifices made it possible for him to succeed.

My siblings and I had the same problem. One day, when my father was talking to his parents on the phone, my brother whispered into his ear, "Dad, tell them in Italian about my being elected to student council."

My father got a pained look on his face. Where could he start? Desolina and Tony had attended one-room schoolhouses until the third grade. Student council? According to Tony, there were hardly enough pencils and sober teachers to go around.

My father tried as best he could. He fumbled through his explanation: "*presidente* . . . . *scuola* . . . *bambini* . . . ." It took about five minutes. After he hung up, my brother asked, "How did you translate 'student council?'"

"Social club."

Some things we didn't bother communicating. News of my Red Cross Life Saving badge was kept quiet because Desolina would have been furious at the thought of my risking my life to save an idiot who swam out too far.

But there were some successes. My sister's ballet accomplishments, accompanied by photos of her in her tutu, were a hit with Tony. Tacked to Desolina's refrigerator was a publicity photo of my brother and the other long-hairs in his band, the Kool-Rays. Desolina used to take it off the fridge and kiss it.

She and Tony owned some shares of Upjohn stock, and she once produced an annual report, turned to a creased page, and asked my father, "*Che cosé?* What is this?"

She pointed to a list of company officers. She'd underlined my father's name so many times her pen had broken through the glossy paper.

"*Sì, sono io,*" my father said. "Yeah, that's me."

"*Te? You? Vice presidente?*" she asked.

"*Sì,*" he said.

She looked up at him and said, "*Non cé male.* Not too bad."

TRAINING

When our family moved to Kalamazoo in 1962, we were told it was for a two-year "training period." The move was traumatic for Desolina. Immigration had separated her from her own family; why was the family being broken up again for the sake of prosperity? Even worse, after the training period ended, my father was asked to stay on and we saw my grandparents about twice a year.

Desolina kept asking, "When are you coming back to New York?"

It was a great source of guilt for my father, but he was a first-generation American. The goal was to strive, get ahead. If it meant leaving family and friends behind, that was the price for you paid for increased prosperity. For Desolina, Astoria was prosperity enough. She continued to query my father about his eventual return, but finally, she gave up.

At my father's retirement party, attended by tens and tens of his colleagues, there were gifts, toasts, and speeches, the last of which was made by my mother.

She said, "As you know, Selvi came here to Kalamazoo from New York City twenty-five years ago. He was told that he would return to New York after two years.

"As you may not know, he is an only-child, and it was very hard for his mother when he left more than twenty-five years ago. So, she has asked me to ask you all, first, 'Is he trained yet?' and, second, 'If not, what's taking so long?'"

NOMI ITALIANI

My wife and I chose the name of our son from a book of Italian names. It was very much unlike the American names our first-generation parents had bestowed on our siblings and us, such as Rebecca, James, George, Gregory, Mark, and Anne. This is the common path. The newly arrived first-generation wants to distance itself from the old country and the old ways; the second generation, now comfortably American, is curious about the old ways and how they continue to shape identity.

We found the name "Luca" simple and handsome. I thought my grandparents, immigrant peasants who landed at Ellis Island in 1929, would have been thrilled with it. I was wrong.

I shared the name with them during a visit a few days after his birth.

"Luca?" Desolina asked. *"Il suo nome è Luca?"*

"Sì," replied, beaming with joy.

She looked at me as if we'd named him Benito Mussolini.

"It's an Italian name," I said in defense.

She snapped her wrist to the left, as if to flick the name from the apartment.

"Mi piace George!" my grandfather hollered from a couch on the other end of the room. where he'd gone to lay, as usual, after our midday meal. "I like George."

"Un bel nome." said Desolina, in dialect. "A beautiful name."

Were they pulling my leg? These old folks had come from families who gave their children names I thought beautifully exotic: Bartolomeo, Dirce, and Scholastica.

"Allora, si chiama Luca," I said, with finality.

Desolina shook hear head, as if there was still plenty of time to change the birth certificate. *"Non, Luca è un nome stupido,"* she said.

Now I was angry. I asked my grandmother, peevishly, "What would *you* name him?"

She took a napkin and pen, wrote something down, and passed it to me.

It said "ENdEI."

I read it several times. I couldn't figure out what she had written.

Desolina had only gone up to the third or fourth grade before her parents pulled her from school to tend the cows. Not only couldn't she spell, but she wrote with an indecipherable mix of capital and lower case letters that reminded me of ransom notes cut from magazines.

"Endee?" I asked.

"ENdEI!" she said.

"Si, Endei," Tony called out. He was looking at us sideways with his head on a pillow. "Very good name."

"Endee?" I asked. "*No capisco.*"

Desolina grabbed the scrap of napkin, took her pen, underlined the word a few times, as if that would help me, and passed it back.

"ENdEI!" she cried. In disgust, she threw down her pen at a plastic banana in the fruit bowl.

I shrugged.

Then my grandfather said it with an inflection that made me understand. "AN-Dei."

"Andy?" I asked.

"*Si!*" they both shouted.

"Andy . . ." I sighed.

"ENdEI," Desolina said.

"*Un bel nome,*" Tony advised.

"I don't like Andy," I said.

"All right, then, George," Desolina said.

I shook my head. "Luca is the boy's name. *Finito.*"

I got up from the table and went to the bathroom to cool off. I was really irritated.

I might've known the name would be a problem. Luca's older sister's name is Alma. Tony and Desolina never got this straight, either. They kept calling her "Elma," which is my mother's name. They could never understand how we could have named Alma something so close to Elma without actually naming her "Elma".

As for Luca, though Desolina adored him, she never took to his name. Either she refused to accept it or, at the age of 91, with her shaky memory, kept forgetting it. Until the day she died she referred to him as "Il Boy."

"*Come sta Il Boy?* How is the boy doing?" or "*E molto intelligente, questo Boy.*"

SEMPLICITÁ

Simplicity

Desolina's inheritance—worth about $61 and change.

FOLLOW THE MONEY

Twice a year, Tony went to the Italian Consulate on Park Avenue and 68th Street in Manhattan to pick up his World War I pension checks. They didn't amount to much—about $160 each. But, he had fought in the trenches and been a POW in Hungary. He wanted what was coming to him.

He'd been drafted at seventeen. When the officers saw his strength and agility, and his propensity to follow orders, they made him a Bersagliere, the Italian equivalent of a U.S. marine. It comes from the verb meaning "to bomb, harass, or badger."

Antonio saw a good deal of action in the trenches during World War I, though he was quick to point out that when an Italian soldier was given the order to charge enemy lines, many commanding officers stayed behind. After all, he said, bitterly, they were recruited from the coddled upper classes. He was finally captured (my hunch at the humiliating Battle of Caporetto, when the Italians lost 40,000 men to death and injury and another 250,000 who surrendered willingly), and was marched eastward for three weeks to a POW camp in Hungary. Under the eye of an especially cruel Italian sergeant who'd sucked up to the enemy, they worked 12-hour days on farms and ate a miserable gruel. He escaped three times and was recaptured twice. The third time he returned to the camp of his own volition because he was starving and could find no quarter with the Hungarian peasants.

He was not released until 1920, two years after the signing of the Armistice and did not return home until 1921. He chalked it up to the ineptitude, not to mention the indifference, of the Italian government. On the day the prisoners heard of their release, they set upon the sergeant when he entered their barracks. The attack turned into a frenzy.

"*Anch'io ci'ho dato un calcio,*" Tony said. "Even I gave him a kick."

It was with the money he'd earned in the army that he used to buy his ship ticket to the United States.

Tony traveled to the consulate by subway. As he got older, my father tried to get him to take cabs, but the old man refused. Why should he spend $20 to pick up a $160 pension check? My father had tried to arrange it so that I could pick up the checks, but the Italians, with uncharacteristic officiousness, insisted that Tony himself show up in the flesh.

When he was 90, Tony developed a temporary but serious problem with his vision. He couldn't see 10 feet in front of him. We had him tested by ophthalmologists, neurosurgeons, and a host of other specialists. It turned out his medications needed adjustment, but for a few weeks we were very worried. I was at their apartment every day to assist with groceries and laundry.

One Saturday morning, as my father was going through a stack of papers, he held up Tony's most recent pension check.

"How did you get Nonno's check?" he asked.

"I didn't get it," I said.

"Did it come in the mail?"

I had been opening their mail every day. I shook my head.

My father looked over at his father lying on the couch. He could stare up at the ceiling for 30 minutes without saying a word.

"Pa, where did you get this check? Did someone go down and get it for you?"

Tony, still looking up at the ceiling, shook his head.

"Did you ask someone from the consulate to bring it by?"

Tony looked at him as if he were a fool. Imagine an Italian functionary coming all the way out to Queens to deliver the check for an ex-peasant soldier.

My father shuddered. With his eyesight hampered, my grandfather would have had to find his way to the elevated on Washington Avenue, climb the steps to the "N" train, take it into Manhattan, make a rather complex change to the Uptown local, get off one stop later at 68th Street, and walk two blocks west. And then make the reverse trip, all the while susceptible to muggers and creeps.

My father asked, with alarm and anger, "Pa, did you go into Manhattan to get this?"

Tony shrugged. This, of course, meant, "How the hell else do you think I got it?"

That was the world my grandparents came from: small and circumscribed and simple, but defined by an insistence on self-sufficiency.

ONE AFTERNOON AT THE PENNA

Tony's sense of self-sufficiency—taking care of all your problems yourself—could go a little too far. One afternoon, my father took his father to get a haircut at the barbershop on Broadway. My father took a seat and thumbed through a magazine. The door opened. The smell of bread from the Parisi Bakery across the street mixed with the scent of hair tonic. A man walked in, greeted the barber, and took a seat next to my father. He cleared his throat.

"Excuse me, is that your father in the chair?" he asked in a low voice.

My father looked up. The newcomer was a middle-aged man with a nondescript face and sporty racetrack clothes that were then popular with men over 50 in Queens. His whisper was conspiratorial.

My father, who never fully expunged the suspicion wrought in his bones while growing up in Hell's Kitchen, shrugged. "Yeah. You know him?"

The man grunted. "I know him, but he doesn't know me."

"What's that?" asked my father, a little impatiently. He laid down the magazine.

"I know him, but he doesn't know me," the man repeated.

My father was going to tell the man to state his business or move on, but before he could do so, the man asked, "How old is he, your father?"

"Eighty-two."

The man smirked.

"Eighty-two . . ." he said, smiling, shaking his head. "He's got a good head of hair for eighty-two. My old man went bald at forty." Then he noticed my father glaring at him and figured it would be the smart thing to end this cryptic talk and say what was on his mind.

"You know the Penna restaurant, around the corner?"

My father nodded.

"I was in there, about five years ago, and your father was having drinks a few stools down from me. He was talking to some guy I never seen, maybe 20 years younger than him. I wasn't paying any attention, and then all of a sudden the other guy calls your father 'a lousy Guinea bastard!' The two started yelling, cursing, and they were shaking their fists. Then the other man got up and went out.

"Your father followed him." The man smirked again, then laughed. "So all of us at the bar rushed over to the window and saw your father had knocked this guy down on the sidewalk and was standing over him with eyes blazing like coals. The man got up and beat it. Your father straightened his sport coat and walked off."

My father sat there, flabbergasted. Finally, he asked, "How long ago did you say this . . ."

"He would have been seventy-seven," the man interrupted, "or thereabouts. What kind of work did he do for a living?"

"Laid terrazzo," my father responded, still in a state of shock.

"Figured. He still had some power left in those arms."

They both looked at Tony. He was staring into the mirror, examining his newly-finished cut. He still had high, sharp-edged cheekbones that gave him an extra mean look when he narrowed his eyes into slits. He nodded his approval to the barber, who removed the cover and shook it out. Tony stood up, paid, and headed towards a hat rack. He hobbled, but had a solid look about him.

The barber signaled to the man that it was his turn. As he got up from his chair, he whispered to my father, "Take good care of him."

THE EYE OF GOD

To avoid his father's wrath, my father had to follow three simple rules: (1) "Never lie to me"; (2) "If I tell you to be home at 9 p.m., it means 9—not 9:01"; and (3) "Stay away from the docks." The docks where ships unloaded on the Hudson were dangerous, filled with all matter of hustlers, plus the Mafia. A teenage boy might be allured by earning some quick money—like standing lookout for a craps game—but he'd soon find himself in over his head.

My grandfather trusted his son, but this didn't mean he didn't check up on him. After supper, on hot summer evenings, Tony went up to the roof to catch a breeze wafting in from the river and smoke Toscano cigar. From this vantage point he could see much of the neighborhood, including the Children's Aid Society playground, where my father hung out.

My father has said that on many occasions, while he was playing basketball, going up for a hook shot, when he was soaring through the air with his arm arched and the ball suspended on his fingertips, he could see, in the distance, his father—cigar hanging from his lower lip and wearing a sleeveless t-shirt that broadcast his muscles—looking down on him like Almighty God.

LOCATION, LOCATION, LOCATION

When Tony and Desolina moved from Hell's Kitchen to Astoria, Tony insisted on keeping their money at the Franklin National Bank, which had no branches outside Manhattan. When my father told him that Queens had plenty of fine banks, Tony shook his head and said, "This is the bank I started with in 1922, and I want to keep my money here."

When my father pointed out the inconvenience of the set up—Tony would have to come all the way into Manhattan to deposit his paychecks—my grandfather again shook his head.

"No, the bank must be in Manhattan."

"Why?" my father asked.

"The money is safer there."

For several years, Tony had to take a 25-minute subway ride to Forty-second Street and Eighth Avenue to execute any transaction. He never complained.

In the early 1960s, he received a letter saying Franklin was closing. He phoned my father and asked what he should do. It was one of the few times he called for help about anything.

A week later, my father accompanied Desolina and Tony, dressed in their finest clothes, to Franklin, had a check made out in the amount of $25,000, and marched from the southwest corner of the intersection to the northeast corner, where a Chase Manhattan was located.

My father was asked to hold onto the check during the journey, though as they crossed the streets, the tension rose:

"*Attenzione a la machina, Selvi!* Watch out for that car!" said Tony.

Desolina clung to my father's arm and asked, "*Quel bus si fermerá per noi?* Is that bus going to stop for us?"

"*Quel uomo sembra un 'bum.' Viene piu vicino á me,*" Tony added. "That guy looks like a bum. Get on the other side of me."

They entered Chase. Tony was so worried he didn't remove his hat.

As they waited for a banker, my father whispered, "Pa, there are plenty of Chase branches in Queens."

The old man said, "Yeah, but the money's safer Manhattan."

SIGNS AND MYSTERIES

Desolina numbered her eggs. I noticed this once when I went looking in the refrigerator for butter. I saw a half dozen eggs in the tray, numbered one to six. She wrote the numbers in blue ink on the shells. I couldn't figure out why. Did she believe someone was sneaking into the apartment to pilfer them, like a fox in a henhouse? But this seemed impossible. Tony and Desolina no longer had company over. All their friends were dead. The only people who came inside were the superintendent, when he needed to repair something, and me.

When I asked my grandmother about the eggs, she waved me off, as if I had discovered a dirty secret and asking about it showed me to be inconsiderate and crass. When I questioned my grandfather, he shrugged, as if he hadn't noticed and didn't give a damn anyway. And so I've been left to ponder this mystery.

Desolina had many funny habits. She liked to write words on scraps of paper. She wrote down things she needed to remember, such as "*Jimmy al vena a mesdi*," to remind her of my arrival at noon. Other times I think she wrote because she had nothing else to do. I would find notes describing the weather: O*ggi piove, domani molto freddo* (today, rain, tomorrow very cold) or she might write her mother's name down on a paper a dozen times *Maria, Maria, Maria, Maria*. I suspect she did this while calling up some memory of her mother.

On one occasion, she gave my father a shopping list that read:

pollo
pane
succo di arancio
zucherro
sale
latte

67

spaghetti
pastene
rubato

My father eyed the list. All the words made sense—chicken, bread, orange juice, sugar—except the last item, *"rubato."*

"Cosa vuol' dire 'rubato'?" he asked. "What is this 'rubato'?"

She slapped her forehead. "Oh yeah," she said. *"Papa l'an ruba, pover uom, tre giorni fa. Martedì.* Papa was robbed, poor man. Three days ago. On Tuesday."

"L'han rubato?!" my father asked, his heart beginning to pound. "He was robbed?!"

"Sì," she said flatly.

It now made sense. The verb "to rob" is *rubare.*

Desolina's memory was iffy at times. She could still remember the birthdays of her six siblings but sometimes couldn't recall what she ate for lunch. She had been afraid she would forget the incident, and she knew that Tony, old warrior that he was, would never tell anyone.

My father, his eyes filling with tears at the thought of some punks rolling his old man, turned to his father, who was sitting on the couch with arms folded.

"Pa, e vero?" he asked. "Pop, is this true?"

My grandfather shrugged. That made it true.

"Pa, tell me what happened," my father insisted.

"They pushed me down and grabbed my money."

"Were you hurt?" asked my father.

"My knee," Tony said, pointing to a knob under his tan slacks. "That's all. The bastards. If only I'd have been 10 years younger."

My father bent down and rolled up Tony's pant leg. A scrape was on its way towards healing. Nevertheless, he was brimming with rage. He felt guilty enough that his parents, now in their late 80s, lived 700 miles from him. He had tried to get them to move to Michigan, but my grandfather refused. Keeping tabs on their life was a struggle. Tony would get sick and not tell anyone until he had to be hospitalized. By the time they'd reached their 90s, my father was flying in every three weeks to check up on them.

There were many surprises. One day he needed to get inside the *baulo* for some family records. The *baulo* was a pine green steamer trunk that my grandmother had used to transport her possessions when she came to New York as a newly married woman in 1930. In addition to papers, it was filled with sheets and pillowcases that she had embroidered during her seven-year wait for my grandfather and which she gave to my mother in dribs and drabs and with great ceremony. There were also photographs and special costume jewelry that she never wore. Some articles were sealed inside an envelope or wrapped in old fabric and sprinkled liberally with camphor.

The *baulo* was in her bedroom, and only she had the key to it. She complained whenever anyone had to get into it, as if it were some high-interest bank account with a penalty for early withdrawals.

Upon relenting, she disappeared in the bedroom and appeared a minute later with the key. Whether she had fetched it from the band of her flesh-toned stocking or from a tiny purse in her closet was anyone's guess. The trunk was then opened, and Desolina hovered over the shoulder of the intruder, usually my father, telling him to stay away from this or that and hurry it up and, c'mon, what the hell are you trying to find we threw it out long ago.

On this occasion, as my father hunted for records so he could fill out federal medical forms, he came across dozens of envelopes, rolled into cylinders and held in place by a rubber band. Curious, he opened one. It held $220. He ripped open another; it contained $60. In a third was a crisp $100 bill.

"C'mon, *basta Selvi, sera il baulo e lasa star tut,*" she said. "Enough. Close the trunk and leave everything alone."

But my father couldn't stop now. All he had to do was reach in and pull out, and he was in possession of two or three more envelopes. Desolina hollered at him, but he continued digging.

My grandmother gave up and took a seat at the kitchen table. Twenty minutes later, my father came out clenching two stacks of envelopes, about fifty in all, and dropped them on the table.

Tony was taking a cat nap, but the sound of envelopes being ripped open awoke him. He got up and tottered over. The table looked like the site of a crap game; there were 20s, 50s, and 100s stacked up, their edges curling, and held in place with a sugar bowl, an ashtray, and wine bottles.

"*Dovet le trova?*" Tony asked. "Where did you find this?"

"*Nel baulo,*" my father said.

"*Nel baulo?!*" Tony hollered, looking up to the heavens. He trained his furious eyes on his wife, who was sitting sheepishly by. "*Ma, porco cane!* What is all this money doing in the house?!"

"*Io non so,* I don't know," she said. "I put it away and forgot about it."

"*Porca vaca!*" he yelled again, fists clenched. "What if the building burned down?!" He turned to my father. "*Cuanti soldi, Selvi?* How much is it?"

"*Io conto,*" my father replied. "I'm still counting."

Desolina was the household keeper of the cash. Every month, Tony took their social security checks, along with his pension money and the occasional check he received from the Italian government as a World War I vet, and cashed them at the bank. He brought the money home, gave it to Desolina, and asked for a few bucks when he needed it.

By the end of the afternoon, $9,600 had been fished out of the *baulo*. Tony was wagging a finger at his wife, who was clasping her hands together and pleading for mercy. Then he got up and paced the floor, crying, "*Nove mille sei cento scudi!* Nine thousand six hundred bucks! *Porca miseria!*"

My father looked at his watch. He had just enough time to get the loot to the bank before it closed. The teller recognized him because he occasionally helped his parents with banking. When she saw $9,600 on the deposit slip, she thought that he'd make a mistake and moved the decimal point one digit to the left. My father tapped on the glass, shook his head, and slid the money—there was no bill smaller than a $20—under the window.

The teller's eyes widened as she counted it. She looked up at him in shock.

"You wouldn't believe it if I told you," my father said.

A year later, when he went fishing in the *baulo* again, he found $1,900.

THE DOWRY

When Desolina's father died, he left the family house, farm implements, and land to his sons. His daughters got $600 each in cash. My grandmother always considered this part of her dowry, despite the fact that she took possession of it nearly thirty years after her marriage, on her only trip back to Italy in 1958. Her sister had been holding it.

She had no idea of what to do with the money until one of her relatives suggested she invest in Italian postal bonds, which were said to be very secure. Desolina promptly took the bus to the post office in Berceto and received three bonds valued at 700,000 lire. After she returned to New York, the bonds were placed in a safe deposit box. They were about 5" x 7" and were imprinted with a handsome peasant, dressed in a crisp shirt and work pants rolled up above sturdy boots, flinging seed into a field from a sling worn around his shoulders.

Thirty-five years later, my father, who'd heard vague rumblings about this dowry, stumbled upon the bonds and brought them to her attention.

"They're worth a lot of money," Desolina said. She rubbed her thumb against her index and middle fingers. "*Molto soldi.* That will be for my great-grandchildren, for college."

My father talked her into cashing them in and investing in something else. She said she would invest in U.S. Savings Bonds.

On his next business trip to Milan, he showed the bonds to a financial analyst at his company, who said he would look into redeeming them.

The next day, the analyst called my father into his office. With great chagrin, my father was informed that, with the devaluation of the lire over the years, the bonds were now worth $184 and change. In addition, because the bonds were so old, they could not be redeemed in Milan. Desolina had bought them in Berceto; they had to be redeemed in Berceto, four hours away by car. There would be many applications to be filled out, with proof that he was truly the son of Desolina *neé* Consigli Vescovi, as well as the pasting of a lot of stamps and the crimping of many official seals for which the Italian bureaucracy is well known.

When my father next saw his mother he explained the situation, but she could not comprehend what devaluation of currency meant. All she knew was that the price of milk, butter, and Canada Dry Ginger Ale went up every year and her bonds should have gone up, too.

She called him "*matto,* crazy," and disappeared into the bedroom, where she locked the door and placed the bonds in the *baulo*.

They remained there until she died. Now they are framed and hanging on the walls of my brother, sister, and me.

STRONGMEN

As a child I used to stare at my grandfather's arms and hands. On his wrist, or perched on his elbow, or under a fingernail, were bits of cement. This was after he had washed up for fifteen minutes at the bathroom sink. Sometimes he missed a few spots. He was always anxious to get to his supper.

Tony laid terrazzo. He did all the jobs of a terrazzo craftsman, but the task he was best at and liked the most was as a "terrazzo helper." The helper mixes the cement and marble chips to create a consistent mixture. A lobby with a first-rate terrazzo floor has a uniformity of marble chips throughout.

My grandfather once walked into a Midtown office building, stopped to look at the workmanship of the floors, and began cursing.

"Too many cracks?" I asked.

He shook his head in disgust. Cracks were unavoidable with any type of flooring. Buildings shifted. It was the inconsistency of the work that angered him. One section was filled with the brown and black chips, while the other had only a sprinkling.

"*Porco cane!*" he muttered, truly disgusted. He wanted to spit on the floor. It was an insult to him and the trade.

Terrazzo work required a lot of muscle. When I used to stare at my grandfather's arms it was not at the cement, but at the muscle underneath. Even adjusting his pinky ring caused the muscles in his forearm to flutter.

Tony was very gentle. He used to play cats cradle with my younger sister. The game bored me, but I used to watch them just to see his strong hands next to her four-year-old mitts.

My grandfather was very modest and quiet, but after a few glasses of wine a jovial, animated side surfaced. He liked to show off. And for him, an afternoon's entertainment might involve a simple feat of strength.

One summer afternoon when my father was ten the family was visited by Piero, a distant cousin. Tony liked Piero a lot and soon after his arrival a bottle of white wine appeared from the ice box. It was Piero's favorite beverage. In his later years when his drinking got bad, Piero's wife filled a wine bottle with urine and set it in the icebox. Piero swallowed a few gulps before he knew what he was drinking; the story made the rounds among all the *paesani*, from The Bronx to Staten Island.

The men drank and talked and drank. They toasted a lot; it was an excuse to empty their glasses. They began arm wrestling. Piero worked in restaurant kitchens, and, though a few inches shorter than Tony, he had a powerful, compact build. After each match, they laughed and had a gulp of wine. When the score was tied 3-3, Piero, as a way of settling the question of who was stronger, informed Tony that he could lift him up in the air over his head.

My grandfather jumped up and dared Piero to try. Piero told him to stand straight as a nail and, on command, fall sideways, remaining stiff. With all the wine Tony had consumed, this was not difficult. He fell into Piero's arms like a falling tree, grinning from ear to ear.

Piero secured his grip and, with a groan, raised Tony shoulder high. After a pause, he grunted and pressed my grandfather into the air. His knees buckled, but it was a good lift. Tony weighed about 180 pounds. My father sat in amazement, though he worried that Piero would drop his drunken father on his head. Piero let Tony down slowly. The two men slapped each other on the back and sat down at the table.

They had another glass of wine. Tony said it was his turn. They got up. Piero went stiff and fell into Tony's arms. Puffing and struggling, my grandfather managed to raise Piero over his head. My father clapped, but Piero did not come immediately down.

Tony began moving his right hand from Piero's buttocks to his lower back. He shimmied his left hand towards the right, until they formed a fulcrum. The room was dead silent.

With a quick jerk, my grandfather pulled away his left hand, so that Piero was suspended by a single arm. My father went bug-eyed. Tony grunted. His knees buckled; Piero didn't remain suspended for long, but it was clear that the feat had been accomplished. Piero came down, his feet hitting the floor with a thump. He and Tony laughed and found their way back to the table and the wine.

IL DOTTORE

My grandparents revered their doctor so much that they didn't like to bring their complaints to him. Desolina would moan about this or that, but when she saw her doctor, she would say, "No, *tutto all right, dottore, grazie.* Everything's fine, thank you."

"But Mama, you told me that your knees hurt," my father said.

"That was two days ago," she replied.

Why bother the doctor? He had enough on his mind. Besides, he might diagnose something really serious.

Their doctor was Umberto Rossini. He ran a shabby office in Astoria, and my father distrusted his medicine. Unlike his young partner, a competent practitioner, Rossini did not keep up with medical developments. He got medicines mixed up. My father tried to get his parents to switch to the younger man, but they shook their heads. Dr. Rossini had kept them healthy, and they would stay with him.

"Rossini, hell," my father told me. "They're still alive by peasant blood and the grace of God."

Examinations by the doctor were very modest. No one completely disrobed. My grandfather would remove his shirt; Dr. Rossini had to listen to Desolina's heart through her dress. Pulse was taken, ankles checked for fluid build up. He might look into their mouths. When he listened to Tony's chest, my grandfather sat up straight like a boy.

One gift Rossini did possess was an ability to detect illness without a thorough examination. He knew the peasant mind.

"So, Signore Vescovi, *come stai?* How do you feel?"

"*Bene. Molto bene, dottore.* Never better in my life."

"*Mangi bene?*" he asked Tony. "Do you eat well?"

"*Si, dottore.*"

"*Dormi bene?* Do you sleep well?"

"*Ma, si.*"

"*Camini tutti I giorni? Esercizio?* Do you walk every day? Exercise?"

"*Tutti I giorni, dottore.*"

While asking these questions Dr. Rossini was giving Tony a good look-over, to see if he could spot any symptom that might signal real trouble.

"*Bravo*, Signore Vescovi." Rossini would give my father a look, as if to say, "He's 92; he's still walking and talking. Let's leave him alone."

Most of what Dr. Rossini did for my grandparents was write prescriptions. Tony was on digitalis for his heart and Lasix for the fluid that built up in his legs. Desolina was on nothing. She was healthy as a horse, despite having several major operations in her life. She used pain to gain attention. One afternoon, she refused to leave Rossini's office without a prescription of her own. The doctor had her describe her symptoms.

Well, she said, there was dizziness, lack of appetite, and general malaise. Rossini listened to her heart, took her pulse. He looked at my father with inquisitive eyes. How far should we take this? Do you want to admit her to Astoria General Hospital for tests? My father had a hunch she was faking. "Lack of appetite" gave it away. Just the other day she had finished his plate of ravioli as well as her own.

"I think we need a prescription," he told Rossini. Out of the corner of his mouth, my father, a pharmaceutical man, said, "placebo."

"*Ah, sì,*" Dr. Rossini said.

He went out and returned with some capsules which had nothing in them.

"Now, Signora Vescovi," he said with gravity, "I want you to take one of these per day for a month. Do not miss a single day. Do you understand me?"

She nodded obediently and later reported to my father that she was feeling much better.

THE TIP

My mother occasionally accompanied my father on his missions to New York, often to handle the activities women like to do together—going to the hairdresser, for example.

The year was 1990. The two women walked a block down 30th Street to a hair salon, where a young man cut, curled, and dried Desolina's hair. She had a scowl on her face the whole time because she was getting the once-over from the ladies who'd entered the salon and were waiting their turn. Desolina never liked being the center of attention unless she was at her best. She stared and clutched her huge pocketbook.

When Desolina was finished, my mother asked the man how much.

"Twelve," he said.

"*Dodici*," my mother said to Desolina.

She opened her pocketbook, reached into the vault, and came up with a five and seven creased singles. She handed it the man and turned around to get her coat.

"Mama, how about a tip?" my mother whispered.

"*Cosa?*"

"*Una mancia.*"

She shrugged.

"Mama, you've got to tip," said my mother.

"I paid him a lot of money already," she insisted.

"Give him something. A little something."

"You do it," she said, putting on he coat. As she was tying her plastic kerchief, she added, "*Dagli venti-cinque soldi.* Give him a quarter."

THE RING

Desolina had an eagle's eye. She could spot a fresh shaving nick from across a room. If you came in with a band-aid on your elbow, she wanted full details about the mishap. She took note of unbuttoned collars, crooked socks, and torn fingernails.

Gina visited once without her wedding ring. The weather was hot and humid, and the ring was giving her a rash.

As we sat down to lunch, Desolina asked her, "*Dov'è il tuo anello?*"

The implication was clear: It was improper for a married woman to be seen without her wedding band.

"I forgot to put it on this morning," Gina lied.

My grandmother ladled out the tortellini, then turned to Gina and asked, "Did you forget to eat breakfast this morning?"

"No," Gina said.

"*Allora, domani, non scordati l'anello,*" she said. "Good. Tomorrow, don't forget the ring."

SEND MONEY HOME

Given the simple existence they led, Tony and Desolina left a scant paper trail marking their lives. The paucity of documentation was the result of two people who were semi-literate, had no checking account, rarely wrote letters, and who tore up every scrap of paper that wasn't serving a purpose.

The papers they did leave behind, however, tell a little something. Among those we found in the *baulo* was the will of my great grandfather, Lorenzo. He left the house, barn, and land to his three sons, on the condition that they give each sister—Scholastica, Maria, Amelia, and Maddalena—1,000 lire. (At that time, the amount was enough to feed a family of four for a month.) He also left 570 lire to his wife, Antonia, to pay her back for money he had borrowed from her dowry. Finally, he asked that 300 lire be set aside for masses to be said for him

The *baulo* also produced receipts for money that Tony sent back to Casaselvatica, his birthplace, during the 1920s. They were in amounts as high as $50. In the post-World War I days the folks back home desperately needed this money, and it was also a way of paying penance for having left the family farm to seek his fortune in America. Lorenzo himself had emigrated to the United States at the turn of the century, but returned home because the air and water made him sick. When my grandfather expressed his intention to emigrate, Lorenzo was strongly against it, but could do nothing to stop him.

We also found evidence that Tony had wired money at least once to Desolina, in the amount of $17.60. It is dated shortly before he returned to Italy. Considering he married her three months after his arrival, the money might have been sent for pre-wedding expenses.

The other documents we found include the following: Tony's sailing papers (his third-class ticket aboard the *Conte Rosso* in 1922;

cost: $85); my father's diphtheria protection card; Tony's WPA card; the by laws of the Mosaic & Terrazzo Union; and a letter from my father on the stationery of the Plaza Athenee Hotel in Paris, dated 1981. Did he write about what it was like to stay in one of the world's finest hotels? No. He wrote of the weather (*pioggia, fresco*; rainy, cool) and took the opportunity to wish his mother a happy birthday.

TONY SLEPT

Tony lived 25 years after his retirement and probably slumbered away 15 of them. He slept 10 hours a night. After lunch, he threw his legs over the arms of his sleeper sofa and dozed for an hour or two. And he catnapped here and there.

We tried to get him into a hobby or some activity. We bought him a subscription to an Italian newspaper, which he used to soak up water that dripped from a radiator. We encouraged him to play bocce; he went twice and gave it up. Bingo was out; he had a fourth grade education and was uncomfortable with numbers. Social clubs were another miss; he was a solitary man. He disliked TV, couldn't understand most of it. When his beloved wrestling disappeared from the airwaves, there was nothing for him to watch.

He had money to treat himself to good wine or a new mattress or visit his sisters in Italy. He refused. He wanted to leave a nest egg behind for his descendants.

"I don't need your money, Pa, enjoy it," my father said.

"You never know," he said, wagging his finger.

Tony spent a lot of time on the stoop. He stared into the foliage of an elm tree. He tipped his Fedora to women with babies. He watched the neighborhood change from Slavs and Italians to Koreans and East-Asian Indians. In his nineties, he became something of a celebrity on the block. He was outside every day, even when the temperature exceeded his age, and could be seen hauling two heavy bags of groceries home.

One afternoon, when we were sitting outside, a cabbie stopped and pulled a lawn chair from the trunk of his car.

"Sir," he said, walking towards Tony, "this is for you." He motioned that he wanted to replace Tony's rickety, shredded lawn chair with the new one.

At the time, I didn't know who the fellow was and begged off, but the man, who wore a pinkish *pugree*, was insistent. He explained that he was a neighbor and worried that Tony's chair was about to collapse. The old man would hurt himself.

We took the chair, and the fellow drove off with a wave.

"You seen him before?" I asked.

Tony shrugged.

In a way, my grandparents never quite comprehended the American moon landing though, ironically, they'd embodied it. As immigrants, they were like the first-stage boosters that propelled a rocket into outer space. Now their mission was over. They should've done like all American retirees: do those things you never had time to do and visit places you'd never visited. The problem was that they had no understanding of retirement. On the farms where they'd grown up, the elderly played useful roles: they tended small gardens, minded toddlers, and told stories when the family gathered at night. Not so in America.

Their situation was part of my reason for attending graduate school in New York. It was also a way to help my father who had a very difficult relationship with his mother. In her eyes, her son deserved to be seated at the right hand of God—sounds advantageous, but it wasn't. He chafed under her pillaging of his affections.

He'd forever displeased her when he'd moved himself and the family 700 miles away to Kalamazoo, Michigan, the site of Upjohn's home office. If you wanted to climb the corporate ladder, that's where you had to go. She never let him hear the end of it. Questions like "When are you coming back?" and words like "abandoned" were flung at him.

But I had nothing to lose. In their eyes, the grandson could do no wrong. For my family, it became a win-win situation. I arrived every week to hugs and sloppy kisses. The table was set with restaurant-ware bowls and short glasses from which we drank red wine. The artificial fruit bowl centerpiece had been moved to the top of the television, next to an assemblage of family portraits. I felt like the happy, big-toothed seven-year-old in one of those photos.

We ate, always in silence. Desolina met any attempt to make conversation with, "Eat now; talk later." After, we adjourned to the stoop and sat. Astoria was a quiet neighborhood. We said little.

Occasionally, I could pull a story or recollection out of them. With Tony, it involved World War I. Desolina spoke about the hard life her family had endured, how she often went hungry, twin siblings who had died of pneumonia after being baptized in the middle of winter. Pulling potatoes and grooming oxen and hauling water was hard work, and it was relentless, she said. Desolina recalled, with a snicker, that her grandmother, with whom she had to share a bed above the barn, snored and hogged the covers.

She always had a comment about the teenagers who strolled by in a romantic embrace, which she viewed as very inappropriate for such a young age. "*Guarda. Hanno le mudante sporche.* Look at that," she said sarcastically. "They're still browning their underwear."

These visits pleased me immensely because they allowed me a taste of what I hope the afterlife will be: the mingling, in one place, of the bodies and spirits of our families, as far back as they go. For a brief moment, I imagined Desolina's snoring grandmother, Genovèffa (b. 1840) and my son, Luca, (b. 1990) in the same room.

SI RICORDIAMO

We Remember

The house in Casaselvatica, parts of which were built in 1609.

Il GIARDINO

On some days he called the land he came from "*il giardino del mondo,* the garden of the world;" on other days, he referred to it as "*un posto bruto,* an ugly place." His dual view was understandable, given the nature of life for Italian peasants in the early 20th century.

Tony's town, Casaselvatica (which means "house of the wild"), had a church and graveyard and a general store that offered few goods. The land, located in the Apennines Mountains, was verdant and hazy in summer, snowbound in winter, and stingy in providing grain and vegetables for its people and animals. The local peasants grew corn, made cheese, and raised chickens, whose eggs were sold at the market. Polenta was eaten often, in bowls for breakfast and roasted for supper. Sugar on a piece of bread made with wheat flour—instead of the chestnut flour that turned bread dark and leaden—was a treat for the children. Children were pulled from school by the third or fourth grade to begin chores such as cleaning stables, feeding chickens, and watering the garden. The girls learned to sew and spin wool and to wash clothes against the rocks in a stream. In the winter, the women punched a hole in the ice by the bank to reach the water. Field work was done by the older boys, men, and oxen. In the dead of winter, when there was little to do, the men went to Sardinia to cut wood. The money was used to buy salt or tobacco or perhaps to pay a doctor.

Young people courted at dances and festivals. If companionship evolved into marriage, two wedding-day feasts were held—one at the home of the bride, the other at the groom's. The dowry was usually a few sheets, pillow cases, and a blanket. The newlyweds moved in with the groom's family and work life began the next day.

At night, people gathered in houses or barns, where animals provided heat, to talk and sing. My grandfather swore that his youngest sister, Maddalena, had such a beautiful voice that she could have sung

87

at Teatro Regio, Parma's famous opera house, if she'd been born to an upper middle class family instead of to farmers. Instead, she sang to the cows.

In seasons when the harvest was poor, it was hard to keep everyone fed. When a chicken cackled, Tony, as a young boy, would rush to the nest before his siblings, poke a hole in the egg, and suck it empty.

After immigrating in 1922, Tony returned twice to Italy: once to marry my grandmother in 1929; and once for a two-month visit in 1958. By the second visit, Tony hardly recognized the place. Many a house, once bursting with family life, was empty. The fields lay mostly fallow because young people had chosen to go to the cities for better paying jobs. Tony had always wanted to be buried in Casaselvatica, but after the 1958 trip he changed his mind. "Nothing's the same," he told my father. "Bury me in America."

Today, Casaselvatica is dead quiet except for the occasional shifting of gears when a Fiat slows down to make a hairpin curve. Then the car races off. All is silence again.

A THOUSAND TORTELLINI

When my grandparents came to visit us in Kalamazoo, among the first things Desolina did after arriving was to set up a tortellini operation in our basement. She was not satisfied, nor would she socialize with anyone, until she had made 1,000 tortellini. She covered two large tables with linen cloths and sprinkled them with flour. In the corner of one table, she propped the dough-making machine and next to it a bowl of the filling, made of eggs, spinach, ricotta and parmgiano cheese, and spices. She called it *pieno*, which means "full" or "crammed".

She rolled out reams and reams of dough. Along them she dropped a daub of *pieno*, doubled the dough over, and cut out the tortellini with a small wooden cupping tool or a shot glass. She laid the finished tortellini out in perfect rows along the flour-dusted tables.

My brother and I brought our friends downstairs to see her work. There she stood, in an old dress with her arms bulging from the short sleeves like procciutto hams. She wore a kerchief on her head. She waved, but didn't say anything. To them she must've seemed like some diorama of a 19th century Italian peasant.

IL VINO

As his father had taught him, my grandfather bottled his wine on a full moon, though he couldn't say why. I later found out that it was believed that the gravitational pull of the full moon compresses sediment and makes for greater clarity and less cloudiness. Either way, he liked his wine.

The process began on a Saturday morning in early fall, when Tony and my father visited grape merchants on the Upper East Side. It was the only time in his life Tony got to play connoisseur, tasting the varieties of grapes and deciding how he would blend them that year. They returned home to Hell's Kitchen and, by noon, a truck showed up with enough grape for 100 bottles of red and 100 bottles of white, plus the mashing machine and some fifty-gallon barrels. Everything was hauled down to a small room in the cellar allotted each tenant for storage.

The grapes, stems and all, were dumped via a funnel and into the machine where, by use of a hand crank, the grapes were turned into juice and pulp. It all went into the barrel which, when filled, had its top nailed down. The barrels were placed on their sides and covered with burlap sacks.

Every so often, Tony descended to the cellar after work and rubbed his palm against the side of each barrel. If it felt too warm, he removed the burlap. If it felt too cool, he threw another sack on.

Two months later, after a quick taste deemed the wine ready, it was bottled at the next full moon. For my teenage father, this was the best part. The wine was sucked from a hose until a natural flow occurred, and bottle after bottle was filled. From time to time, between bottles, he and Tony sipped. The bottles were corked with a machine delivered by the grape company, though not before Tony gave the corks a glazing of olive oil to ease them in. (The remaining mash was used to make grappa, which is made by distilling the skins, pulp, seeds, and stems left over from winemaking.) They would both emerge from the cellar, feeling no pain, much to Desolina's disapproval.

BRISCOLA

Hold your hand in a fist. Stick out your thumb and pinky, so that your hand looks like a fat bird with tiny wings. Now, pivoting at your wrist, shake your hand back and forth, so that the wings flutter.

Members of my family use this sign regularly. Among Italians, it means "bullshit." The more intense the flutter, the bigger the bullshit. Once a man was telling my father and mother about a harrowing landing he had made while a passenger on a 747. The huge jet had had to make an emergency landing at a podunk airport whose runways couldn't handle the weight of large jets. As the plane lurched right and left, it was actually tearing up the runway in its tracks. My father nudged my mother's knee, brought his hand up to his belt, and fluttered under the table. As the story continued, the fluttering got so wild that my father's hand looked like it was surging with electricity.

Hand and facial signs are common in Italian family life. My grandfather, a man of few words, had a way of extending his lower lip and nodding his head at the end of a story or an outlandish claim. I am not sure whether he got it from Mussolini or vice versa, but it meant, "It's one hundred percent true, and you can look it up."

My grandmother used to raise her hand and make a chopping motion. This meant many things, such as "Watch out, you're going to get it," or "Wow, isn't that wonderful." She frequently made the chop as I came through the door of her apartment. It meant, "It's about time; it's been too long since your last visit." When I departed, the chop meant, "Why are you leaving so soon?"

When I was a boy, she taught me signals connected to a card game she'd learned back in Italy, called Briscola. They were actually facial gestures and were against the rules, but she didn't care because she wanted to win at any cost. After meals, she got out the cards and rounded up a foursome. She liked to play fast. If you paused over your cards for two seconds, she would ask, "*Oggi o domani?* Today or tomorrow?" She insisted on keeping score. What was the point of playing if a winner couldn't be declared?

The word "Briscola" means "trump." A simple card game, it is most exciting when four people play on two teams. No talking is permitted during the first hand. After that, players can communicate, but only in vague terms. A player can say, "I have a high Briscola" or he can ask his partner, "Can you play a card with high points?" but players may never mention that they are holding a specific card.

One afternoon, in a foursome against my grandfather and brother, Desolina got my attention by kicking my shoe. She shifted her eyes back and forth to make sure our opponents weren't watching and then noiselessly puckered her lips several times. She was a very affectionate lady, and I thought she was blowing me a kiss. I puckered back, though making a kissing sound. My grandfather looked up; he knew what she was up to, and he gave her the evil eye. The game proceeded without further puckering.

She later explained to me what she was doing. Yes, she loved me, but she was not blowing a kiss during Briscola. That was neither the time nor place for displays of affection. Her puckering was the signal that she was holding the ace of the Briscola.

There were other signals, she explained. If you had the Briscola three, the second most powerful card in the deck, you twitched your lip twice. If you held the king, you raised your eyes subtly towards the ceiling, as if a rain drop had just landed on your forehead. For the Briscola queen, you gave your shoulder a twitch. This was the least subtle and therefore the riskiest gesture. Once, after my grandfather caught Desolina doing it, he turned to her and said, "What's the matter with you?! Got fleas?!" and he began moving his shoulders wildly about as if he had St. Vitus's dance. Of course, there was a signal to signal to your partner that your opponents were using signals. This was done by stroking the side of your nose with your index finger.

Our Briscola games went on for hours. Then we went outside for a sit on the stoop and came back in and ate supper. Then we played again. Desolina, who dealt from the bottom of the deck, was, like me, intensely competitive. Before every game, she'd look at her partner, slap the side of her leg, and say, "*In gamba.*" Literally, it means, "in the leg"; figuratively, it means "be smart; get on the ball; or don't screw up." She kept score on the back of envelopes and on scraps of paper. We played with an American Airlines deck she got on one of three flights she ever took.

When I was young and saw them only once or twice a year, we would pick up where we left off. We hugged, we ate, and out came the cards. Sometimes Desolina would be keeping score on the reverse side of a scrap we'd used the year before.

ROOM WITH A VIEW

In 1987, my wife, Gina, and I honeymooned in Europe and stayed several days with my great uncle and aunt, Domenico and Ermina, in the old family house. We arrived on a cool September evening, having hitchhiked from Berceto because we had missed the last bus. I was hoping for the chance to show off my rudimentary Italian, but when I began bantering, the driver said, "*Nein, nein.* I am German." He told us, in perfect English, that he was vacationing in the area, which was becoming very popular with his countrymen, who were buying up and refurbishing old peasant houses.

When I later told Ermina about him, she shook her head.

"The last time the Germans were here they stormed into the house looking for partisans," she said, referring to the waning days of World War II, as the Germans retreated northward.

After we passed a battered, leaning sign that said CASASELVATICA, I directed our driver down a lane lined with dilapidated barns, chicken coops, and houses, whose shutters were battened down so that hardly a crack of light was visible.

"Arrivederci!" the German called out to us as he drove off.

We stood with our backpacks before green double doors of the Vescovi home. The lintel was less than six feet off the ground. I knocked. We waited. I knocked again. Finally, we heard slippers shuffling on a stone floor. The door was flung open, and Zio Domenico, who was an exact miniature likeness of Tony, eyed us with a cigarette hanging off his lower lip. It had been many years since he'd seen me as a long-haired college junior touring Europe—plus he was looking at us through a haze of pinot grigio, his favorite beverage—but soon enough he pulled us inside and there were many hugs and kisses.

We were led into the kitchen where Zia Ermina had been knitting. It was clear that she and my uncle had been sitting there the whole time we had been knocking, but had not responded. It was peasant behavior. You didn't answer a knock outside of certain hours unless it was persistent. That meant it was for you, instead of being the arrival of trouble that belonged to someone else.

Ermina was a small woman with broad shoulders and reddish gray hair. She was chatty and wrung her hands when she spoke. There was a continuous twinkle in her eye that wavered between sparks of joy and a glowing coal of nebulous anxiety.

"I am sorry you had to wait in the cold," she said. "We were expecting you, but the day was vague . . ." We had written to say we would be arriving on a Wednesday or Thursday. Casaselvatica is not the easiest place in the world to get to.

We sat down at the table. The kitchen was spare, but modern. There was a stove, a small refrigerator, and a fireplace. The sink was located in an adjoining room and was made of stone. Ermina brought out bread and prune jam and heated bowls of steaming milk.

We relayed news of my grandparents, which made Domenico weep. Just the mention of his brother's name was enough to cause a flood of tears. The fact that he'd seen Tony only once since 1922 was a cause of great pain. During our stay, he let it be known that he'd felt abandoned by his two older brothers, who had emigrated when he was not yet ten years old.

Ermina was anxious to get us upstairs. She brought us into the bedroom, which had served as the quarters for Tony and Desolina before they came to the United States. Delicate blue flowers had been painted on the walls.

She asked me, "When was your father was born?"

"June, 1930."

"Ahhhh," she said, while turning down the bed cover, and told me in a round about way that he'd been conceived in this room and hoped we had the same fertile luck.

Gina and I went to bed under a thick layer of covers. With the shutters closed—and they were to remain closed until morning, Ermina told us—the room was pitch black.

In the morning, I jumped out of bed and threw them open. The countryside was verdant, a green that glowed from a heavy night drizzle. White clouds with gray beards scudded across the mountaintops. Where you could see snatches of sky it was a purple.

Gina came onto my side. I made her crook her neck and she could just see Casalasagna, Desolina's village.

Ermina called us down for breakfast. We ate more bread, prune jam, and milk, and she cut up some apples, whose peelings she burned to scent the air.

CASALASAGNA

Desolina grew up in a hamlet called Casalasagna, which means House of Lasagna. It was simply a cluster of houses without any church or store. She could not explain to me how the place got that name. When asked, she would shrug her shoulders and roll her eyes. This meant either she had no idea or that the name's meaning was obvious (someone in the town's history made extraordinary lasagna). She came from a large family and, because there was not enough space in the house, she slept in a room over the barn with her grandmother. The old woman used to hog the bed, Desolina used to say, but she was glad to be sleeping in a place that was warmed by the heat from the cows and pigs below.

One of my grandmother's jobs in her youth was bringing the cows up the mountain to pasture land. It was a tedious job. All day long she had nothing to do but keep an eye on the dumb beasts and watch the clouds scrape their white bellies across Mount Cervillino. Lunch was a piece of cheese with bread or a hunk of polenta left over from the morning. An occasional cowbell broke her reverie.

It was also broken by my grandfather, who rode his bike to her house and, when possible, took her around on the handlebars.

I asked him, "How did you court in those days?"

"What do you mean, How did we court? How did *you* court?" he asked. "Do I ask you about your business?"

Desolina was still guarding the cows when Tony left for the United States. She would rush the cows home to see whether a letter came from him. Tony was not a prolific writer, but his letters arrived often enough to keep their romance kindled. Every week she wrote him and got money for a stamp from her mother, who told her she was foolish to await his return.

The correspondence paid off. He returned an American citizen, and they were married in February 1929. She moved into his house and, when they embarked for America in 1930, she was five months pregnant.

When my wife and I visited Casalasagna, the house belonged to another family and the barn was falling apart. There were holes in the ceiling and hay and broken tools lay scattered about. I entered anyway and climbed a rickety staircase to the upper level. A cold September wind whipped through crumbling structure. I made my way across rafters, under which Desolina and my great, great grandmother had slept. I found the rusty blade of a scythe. I lowered it down to my wife. Before we left Italy, we wrapped its nicked blade in black tape, packed it in a box, and mailed it home, where it hangs in my father's house.

THE FAMILY ESTATE

During my honeymoon Domenico took me for a walk to show me the Vescovi land. We owned no property near the house, except for a small patch across the road that had been used to grow corn. Now it lay fallow. It couldn't have been bigger than 200 x 200 feet.

We walked along the main road, past a factory that made Parmesan cheese, and turned off on a rutted lane that wound its way past trees, fields, and farm buildings, inside of which old men were tinkering.

Zio Domenico stopped, surveyed the area with slow 360-degree turn, and said, "There! We own that!"

"Where?" I asked. I couldn't tell what he was pointing at.

"The land between this tree by the road and that corner of that old house, and from that house to that fence post and from the post to the stream."

The plot wasn't much bigger than the one by the house.

The day was cool and overcast. Up the mountain we went, with Domenico waving vaguely to the right and to the left: "We own that, from the stump to the water well and down past the lane, but not including that barn," and "That belongs to the Capra family over there," and "Over there, see it? That's ours. From this garden to that pasture beyond those trees."

Some of the parcels had trapezoidal shapes, others had so many twists and turns they looked like gerrymandered congressional districts. It was all fallow, and not one tract would have amounted to a respectable family farm by American standards.

"Why don't we own one big piece?" I finally asked him. "Wouldn't it have been easier?"

Cigarette hanging from his lip, Domenico looked at me while trying to suppress disgust.

"The land is very old here, *nipote*," he said, striking a match. "Families had to acquire it a little at a time. Some of the land was used for farming, others to graze animals, and, up high, for wood to heat the house."

We arrived at a hamlet where Zio said we would have "*un bicchiere*," literally, "a glass," meaning a glass of wine or liquor. We knocked on the door of a friend and soon we were sitting at the table drinking Pinot. My uncle and his friend, whose good looks were eroded by his stubbled face and shabby dress, launched into a harangue about how swell life had been in the old days. The region had once been vibrant; now, with everyone gone for the cities, it was like a ghost town, they said. Only old people remained. The cafés kept irregular hours. There was nothing to buy on the shelves of the general stores.

After a few glasses, we headed home. Zio sped up when our house came into view and disappeared into the barn. I arrived just as he emerged, struggling with his zipper.

"That was close," he said.

"Why don't you use the toilet in the house?" I asked. Indoor plumbing had been installed several years earlier.

He was standing under the lintel, into which was carved the date of the house: 1609. He said, "Sometimes I just want to use the old one, damn it."

THE DRESS

Before I left for my honeymoon, Desolina told me several times to look for *la vesta*, the dress. She had left it behind during her last visit in 1958. She gave me the precise location: third floor, first room to the left, oak armoire. The dress itself was green. She emphasized that I had to get up to see it without her sister-in-law, Ermina, knowing about it.

"Do you want me to bring it back?" I asked.

"No, no, no!" she said. "Just make sure it's there."

Leaving the dress was Desolina's way of asserting her rights: a third of the house still belonged to Antonio Vescovi, despite the fact that he lived 3,500 miles away.

I wanted to do more for my grandparents than skulk around in search of a dress. I asked my grandfather if there was anyone we should visit for him, or could we perhaps take something over?

No, there were no messages or treasures to deliver, he said. "Just say hello to everybody."

"*E la vesta*," said Desolina. "*Non scordarti.* Don't forget."

When I told my father about the special mission, he said, "Watch out for Ermina. These old peasants have eyes in the back of their heads."

The most interesting person Gina and I had met on our trip was Elena. She had noticed us lingering around the church one morning. After I identified myself and my origins, she broke into a smile. Of course she knew Tony and Desolina Vescovi, she said. Her own mother—the best cook in the village—had prepared their wedding feast. Elena invited us into her home for espresso and cookies. She was gracious, funny, and very intelligent. What was most intriguing was her gender, which we couldn't make out.

Elena had the broad shoulders and large hands of a man, as well as a light mustache, but she also possessed slender wrists and delicate

102

calves. Her voice was very deep, but she wore a dress and stockings and identified herself as a woman. She was very evasive when entertaining questions that would hint at her gender. When I asked her if she had children, she responded, "The mountains are my children."

Ermina and Domenico had turned red-faced when I had mentioned our visit with Elena. They didn't want to talk about her.

A week after Gina and I arrived back in New York, we went to Astoria to recount the trip. Friends of my grandparents had given us gifts, not to mention countless hugs and greetings. A letter from one of Tony's childhood friends made him weep like a baby.

"Oh, and by the way, we saw Elena," I said. "Remember her? Her mother cooked your wedding dinner."

As soon as they heard her name, my grandparents sat up straight.

At the same time they said, Tony: "She's a strong woman;" Desolina: "Poor man."

As Gina and I were leaving, Desolina pulled me aside and whispered, "*La vesta, l' era la?* The dress, was it there?"

It was.

STARE PER FINIRE

Beginning of the End

Tony with the author's daughter, Alma, in 1988.

GET OFF THE PHONE

As my grandparents got older, my father came to see them with increased regularity. It wasn't that he didn't trust me. But they were his parents and, ultimately, his responsibility, which he took very seriously. His visits made for some fractious situations.

One day, just before the four of us sat down for lunch, he got a business call. We waited and waited for his return to the table. The phone was down the hall. I could hear snatches of the conversation. It was not going to be a short call.

"Let's eat," I said, reaching for a soup ladle.

Desolina gave me an icy look.

"C'mon!" Tony finally said, waving away my grandmother's etiquette as if it were a cloud of flies. "*Mangiamo!*"

Desolina got up and shuffled to the end of the hallway. My father was at the other end, with a black rotary phone in the crook of his shoulder. She got his attention and pointed to her watch.

"C'mon. *Aspetema!* We're waiting for you," she said in a piercing whisper. "*Mangiamo!*"

My father was annoyed not only about the stupid actions that had precipitated this call, but about the cord on this boxy old unit, which was not long enough to stretch to a flat surface. He had to write against a wall and his pen went dry every ten seconds.

She waved at him again and pointed to her mouth.

He angrily swatted the air, a gesture that we should start eating without him.

Desolina returned to the table.

"*Mangiamo,*" she said with resignation.

I dished out the soup, and we ate in silence, except for the sound of my father's voice, which got louder and more intense.

Desolina finished well before anyone else. She got up and poked her head into the hallway.

"C'mon Selvi," she called. "*Basta parlare! A tavola!* Enough talking! Come to the table!"

My father was on a conference call with colleagues in Dallas, San Jose, and Cleveland. They were talking about investor confidence and potential lawsuits. *The Wall Street Journal* had called wanting a comment. To Desolina, he was blabbing away, using up time that could be spent with her.

I got up and prodded her back to the table. She slumped in her chair and said, "Tony, give me a few more cappelletti."

By the time we'd finished the second round, my father had been away twenty minutes. Tony, stoic as ever, reached for an apple and began slicing it into wedges, which he ate off the tip of the knife. After that, he'd have dessert and hit the sofa for his post-lunch siesta.

Desolina stewed at the lost opportunity to eat with her son who, in her eyes, came so infrequently. She shoved back her chair and returned to the hall, waving her arms like a football referee signaling the end of a play. When she got no rise out of my father, she turned around and asked me, "*Ma, cosal parla per tant taimp?* What could he be talking about for so long?"

It was an honest question. A long telephone call was impossible to explain to her. Her calls never lasted more than three minutes. Besides, for Desolina, when it was time to eat, you put down the plow or stopped milking the cows and came to the table.

"Selvi, *mangi oggi o domani?!* Are you going to eat today or tomorrow?!" she hollered sarcastically.

My father turned his back on her. Had she been within distance, he might've tried to strangle her with the cord. Poor man, he lived a double life, one hand washing the floors in his mother's home, the other attempting to clean up some corporate crisis. It was more than one generation could hold.

Desolina grabbed the switch and began flicking the light on and off, on and off, on and off. Scribbling away, my father looked up at me for help. It took me ten seconds to pry her fingers loose and lure her back to the table for Entenmann's pound cake.

MR. CLEAN

When my grandparents reached their nineties my father hired a young Colombian woman who lived down the hall to check up on them daily and do their laundry. She was very kind. She spoke to them in Spanish. They replied in Italian. The languages were close enough.

However, the important work, and the dirty work, fell to my father. He insisted on it. He flew in from Michigan to escort his parents to doctor's appointments, washed their hair, clipped their toenails, and regulated their medicine. He threw himself into the work as if $50 million worth of business was on the line. In fact, there was a considerable amount of pressure in this new job. He was not beholden to stockholders, but to Desolina.

My father spent his life trying to break free from her hold. His first emancipation occurred when he was thirteen when she went to slap him across the face. His threw up his arm and blocked her blow. She grabbed her forearm and screamed out in pain. He walked out of the apartment. She never tried to strike him again.

Even as he broke away from her orbit, he remained a dutiful son. I would often arrive at the apartment in Astoria to find him up to his ears in mops, buckets, and rags. If it were a hot summer day, he'd be attired in old shorts and a t-shirt, and have a kerchief around his head His body was glazed with sweat, as if he'd just stepped out of a sauna.

"*Ma, caro figlio*, but dear son, why do you come half way across the country to clean like this?" Desolina asked him. She'd be sitting comfortably watching him work. "Wouldn't it be easier for all of us to live near each other? Now that you're retired, why don't you come back to New York?"

My father would have cleaned a thousand baking apartments before agreeing to her request.

"No, Mama, you're better off in your own home, where you know where everything is," he replied.

Desolina chewed on that notion for a few moments. She wasn't stupid. She knew he didn't want to live under the same roof.

"O.K., then go to it," she would say, waving her hand at the cleaning supplies. "And by the way, you missed a spot over there in the corner of the floor."

VIEW FROM THE STOOP

One day after lunch my grandparents and I went outside to find a Cadillac hearse double-parked in front of the next building. The building door opened and a group of weeping Filipino women between ten and fifty years old appeared. On their heels came a man walking backwards, the front of a walnut coffin in his hands. He was middle-aged and wore a black leather jacket. After he nearly tripped down the steps of the stoop, he cursed a man carrying the coffin's other end, a guy in a New York Jets jersey. They worked the casket between two parked cars and towards the hearse.

We watched from our lawn chairs on the sidewalk. Tony gave the scene a quick glance and turned away. It took Desolina longer to take everything in. After she'd understood, she nudged me and crossed herself. Fumbling and cursing, the undertakers finally slid the box in the car and closed the double doors, which triggered more crying from the women. They watched the men climb in the hearse—acting more like a deliverymen who'd come to fetch a mattress a buyer had found unsatisfactory—and drive off. In a weeping herd, the women went back inside their building.

Desolina looked at me and shrugged, as if to say, "Well, what can you to do?"

I studied my grandfather, 91 at the time. He'd closed his eyes to doze. I wondered if the drama had any effect on him—perhaps reminded him that his ride in a wooden box couldn't be more than a few years away. But, no, he was as taciturn as ever.

We sat some more. Desolina adjusted her garter several times. Tony sat so still I watched the front of his flannel shirt to make sure he was breathing.

And then, as if an alarm went off, they stood up and rubbed their arms to spur circulation. It was time for a snack and a few hands of Briscola. We headed up the stoop. My grandmother halted halfway and turned to the place where the bereaved had been standing and crying, but the pause, I think, was just to catch her breath.

THE SLEEP-OVER

Around his 91st birthday, my grandfather got sick and had to be hospitalized with fluid in his lungs. I had him admitted to Astoria General while my wife stayed with Desolina at the apartment. Tony, who ignored his ailments and never flinched when physicians came towards him with needles, got a worried look on his face as I prepared to depart.

He motioned me over to his bed.

"What do I do with this?" he asked.

In his hand was $1,000 in cash, which he had brought along to pay the hospital bill, as well any special sundries and services.

"Let me take it. They have a safe here," I said, and when he didn't understand, I added: "*una banca del ospedale.*"

He released the bills and I put them in my pocket. I found a men's room and stuffed the cash in my sock.

When I arrived back at the apartment, Gina and my grandmother were seated in silence at the kitchen table. Gina was stroking Desolina's hand.

"*Tutto all right, il babbo?*" Desolina asked me. "Is everything all right with Papa?"

"*Bene,*" I said.

"Then why isn't he with you?" she asked.

"He has to stay in the hospital for a few days," I replied. "Don't worry."

She looked up at the heavens and gave the chopping motion with her hand.

"I'm going to stay with you tonight," Gina said.

Desolina's face lit up, as if she were thinking, "Hey, this could be fun." She gave Gina a hug and a kiss.

I said my good-nights and left, promising to call the next day with news of Tony.

There was the sleeper-sofa Tony slept on, but it seemed inappropriate for Gina to take it. There was also a couch, but Desolina wouldn't have her sleeping there. The girls would spend the night in her bed.

Desolina prepared her nightly snack, a bowl of warm milk and anisette toast, got into her sleep wear, a faded house dress and kerchief, and climbed into bed. Gina put on an old nightgown, turned off the light and slipped between the covers. Desolina's hand clasped hers. A few moments later, she was snoring away.

Outside there was still enough light so that a group of boys could play stickball. People talked on the stoop.

When Gina awoke in the morning, Desolina's side of the bed was empty. She sat up and pulled the shade to one side. The grey light of dawn had just broken. She heard Desolina coming and lay back down, pretending to sleep. My grandmother entered the bedroom and began banging drawers and sighing. The moment Gina opened her eyes Desolina threw her a kiss.

"Eat," she whispered.

They went down the hall to the kitchen for breakfast, warm milk and anisette toast. They ate at a small table below a shelf holding a bust of the Virgin Mary and a vase with plastic flowers. Outside, the alley was still dark. When they'd finished, the clock read 7:10 a.m. They cleared and washed the dishes. It was awkward. Two people were not required for such a task. Gina went to the bedroom to get dressed. Desolina paced the hallway, the wood creaking under the linoleum, anxiously eyeing the phone that hung on the wall, waiting for my call from the hospital.

PATRIMONY

One Christmas my father gave me Philip Roth's *Patrimony*, the story of the relationship between the author and his father, Herman, during the latter's dying days. In one passage, which my father had spoken about, Roth stumbles upon his 86-year-old father in the bathroom. Roth writes: "At the sight of me he came close to bursting into tears. 'I beshat myself,' he said. There is [excrement] all over the bathroom, on the floor, walls, mirror." As Roth gently helps his father get cleaned up, the old man repeats, "I beshat myself!" and this time dissolves into tears.

Within a year, my father was facing the same trials as the author. He was helping his parents with hygiene, washing behind ears, giving haircuts. On more than one occasion, he had to hurry them home from the Sanford Diner. Most of the time they made it, occasionally they didn't.

One day I was visiting my grandfather in the hospital when he soiled himself. I called a nurse; she said she'd attend to it. After 15 minutes, I decided to do it myself.

"Roll over, Nonno, let me help you," I said, reaching for a basin and soap.

He shook his head, then slowly raised his index finger, wagging it back and forth, and said, "You can't do that kinda business."

It was so. A grandson couldn't; a son had no choice.

TUTTO 'FREE'

Even between my father and me and the Colombian lady doing piecemeal care, my grandparents' independence couldn't last forever. Tony and Desolina's diet was going to pot. Their medical conditions needed supervision. There came a day when allowing them to live alone would have amounted to negligence.

My father decided he had to bring them to an assisted-living facility in Kalamazoo. It was not going to be easy. "Assisted-living" was a concept most Americans didn't understand at the time, let alone Tony and Desolina. In their eyes, any residence for old people was a nursing home, and this set off fireworks. My grandfather despised such places.

My father had tried to get them to move years earlier, with hurtful consequences. When he showed his father brochures of a clean, comfortable place, Tony went berserk. He jumped up from the dining table. His eyes were blazing.

"This is where people go to die!" he yelled. "You're trying to put me and Mama in a place like that?!" He took a menacing step towards my father. "I'll go in there over my dead body."

But today was different. The two of them were nearing their mid-nineties.

My father sat them both down at the table. He explained how an assisted-living facility was different from a nursing home. He showed them brochures with photos of an elegant dining room and outdoor garden. He swore to them on a stack of bibles that he had seen the place, and it was clean and well operated.

"No, I'm not going," Desolina jumped in. "I'm too old to get on a plane and move to Kalamazoo."

My father was surprised. Desolina would have lived in hell if it brought her closer to her son. But, then again, she had always been unpredictable.

"But Mama, the flight is only two hours long. *É un bel posto!* And it's such a beautiful place. Look at the dining room. *Hanno il 'ros bif' tutte le Domeniche.* They serve prime rib every Sunday. And I live five minutes away."

Desolina shook her head.

"There are four meals a day! Breakfast, lunch, dinner, and *un spuntino prima di dormire!* A snack before bedtime!" he pleaded.

Desolina grunted in the negative. "No, Selvi, it's time for you to come back here to take care of us." She folded her arms and sat back in her chair.

My father now tried to work on Tony, who shook his head adamantly. He didn't want to live under anyone else's thumb. These places served lousy food. And they were expensive. As a last resort, he banked on Tony's sense out of duty. He pointed out that Desolina really needed help and that he, Tony, could no longer provide it. It behooved him to think of his wife.

Tears came to Tony's eyes. He knew it was true. It was the end of an era. He had lived in New York for seventy years and on that block in Astoria for forty. It was time to go. He wept.

My father now had to tip the scale and get Tony to say "yes." He accomplished this with a lie.

"And Pa, you're not going to believe it, but the place is free."

Tony wiped his eyes and looked up.

"*E* free?"

"*Si.*"

"*Ma, no!*" Tony said.

"*Si.*"

"*Ma, chi paga?* Who pays for this?"

"My company. It's one of the benefits I get. I don't need the place now, but my parents are allowed to stay there. For free."

"*E vero?*" he asked. "Is this true?"

My father nodded. "*Tutto* free. Everything is free."

Tony couldn't stop shaking his head.

Desolina, who was growing more and more deaf in her old age, leaned forward and asked: "What are you people talking about? *E al Papa, perche al pianza?* And why is Papa crying?"

"*Porco cane,* free!" said Tony. "*Che compagnia!* God bless America!"

"Then you'll go? It really is a beautiful place, Pa," my father said.

Tony sighed. "All right," he said, and the tears came again.

"*Selvi, perche piange il Babbo?* Why is Papa crying?" Desolina asked again.

"He said he'll come to Kalamazoo," my father replied.

"*No*," she said. "*E vero?*"

My father nodded.

"Tony," she said to him across the table. "*At ve a Kalamazoo?*

He nodded.

Desolina looked at her son. "*Se va il Babbo, vengo anch'io.* Well, if he's going, I'm going, too."

And so on a hot August day, Tony and Desolina flew first class with my father to Kalamazoo. My mother met them at the airport and chauffeured them to Director's Hall, an assisted-living residence for 200 people. Tony and Desolina—at ninety-four and ninety three—were not even the oldest couple in the place.

Settling these two old peasants into their new surroundings was touch and go. Accepting scheduled baths and nurse visits was not easy. Hard as they tried, the aides could not get them down to the arts and crafts center or to chapel. Mostly, Tony and Desolina stayed in their room, watched TV, and waited for daily visits from my mother. They got the routines down. Tony grew fond of the place—the food, the gardens, the nice people.

He would sit in the dining room, his plate heaped with food, and aides serving all the iced tea he wanted. The chairs were soft, the carpet plush.

On my first visit, he looked at me with wonder and said, "Jimmy, *chi paga per questa roba?* Who pays for all this stuff around here?"

"*É* free," I said.

OLD WORLD GRIEF

Tony died several months after moving into the assisted care residence. Some kind of cancer, we think. We did few tests and stopped. It wasn't worth putting him through the pain and fear. It was his time to go.

"*Un bel posto,*" he'd said, of the residence. "A beautiful place." He was glad he had come. My father sometimes found him sitting in a sunny courtyard stroking the resident cat.

The day after his death the weather turned brutally cold. The daytime highs hovered around 9 degrees. We bundled Desolina up and brought her to the funeral home.

The moment she saw her husband laid out, she broke away from my father and rushed up to the casket. She gripped the sides and began wailing. There were no other visitors in the room. Tony and Desolina had outlived all their friends and hadn't made any new ones in Kalamazoo. To fill the void, my father had invited some of his business colleagues, but they hadn't arrived yet. She wailed and wailed, drowning out the sound of the home's saccharine music.

My father tried to escort her away, but Desolina wouldn't budge. She jammed her palm in her mouth and bit it. She looked up at the heavens and wailed.

A funeral director haltingly approached me to make sure everything was to our satisfaction.

Yes, I told him, everything was fine. Tony looked good, his favorite Barney's suit as spiffy as it had ever been. Desolina was mourning as she wanted.

We finally got her to a couch, where she sat and cried some more and made an occasional dash for the casket. She finally calmed herself down. She repeated to herself what a good man he had been, and we agreed with her. Her breathing slowed. She sank into the couch. Her face lit up when my father's colleagues arrived. I could see him gritting his teeth, hoping she wouldn't implode again.

Desolina behaved. In fact, she was quite charming. When it was time to go, she wailed again, but no one expected anything less. We finally tugged her away from the casket. Her steps, as we headed for the car, got more and more firm. No more crumbling at the knees for Desolina. Yes, Tony was a good man, but it was time to move on.

When someone died in Hell's Kitchen, even if you knew the deceased only in passing, you went to the wake. It was a chance to catch up with friends. After you knelt at the bier and paid your respects to the family, the objective became socializing. You sought out former neighbors to find out how they liked living on Long Island, or went looking for a third cousin who owed you money.

Except with close family, it was also the custom among mourners to *marcare un posto* (mark a place). That meant you put some money down for a place in one of the limousines going to the cemetery on the day of the funeral, but then let it be known that you were not going to the cemetery. The money ended up in the pocket of the family to help cover burial expenses.

Only one limousine was needed for Tony's ride to the cemetery. Before we left from the funeral home, we conducted our own service, which consisted of prayers and the story of Don Dante, the only priest I'd ever heard Tony speak of. Don Dante, he told me with tears in his eyes, was a priest from one of the hill towns around Berceto who had traveled to a stinking, rotting prison in Southern Italy to retrieve a local boy who had deserted the army in World War I. Here was a man of God, Tony said, not like the priests who stole from the poor box. This man represented the summation of Tony's religious life. Don Dante was Christ in the flesh to him.

We bundled ourselves up and the two-car procession headed to the cemetery. The roads were glazed with snow. We stood at the grave site under an awning snapping in the frigid wind. It was too cold to bring Desolina. The grave diggers hovered nearby. My father made it quick; he told us all how much Tony loved us and thanked us for our love for him. He gave us each an embrace.

He approached me last, placing my frigid cheeks in his gloved hands and gazing, watery eyes into watery eyes.

"And now let's go home and celebrate his life and eat the way he would have wanted us to eat," he said.

At dinner, we toasted Tony's life, his union, and his pharmacist. After dessert, we opened wine that he and my father had bottled in the 1940s in the cellar on 39th Street. Even as we poured the stuff we could tell it was no good. The cork had crumbled into the wine, whose consistency was styrated, but we all had a sip. It was bitter, but it felt good and right to roll a few drops around our tongues and swallow.

THE DAILY ROUTINE

Residents at the assisted living home ate at tables of four, though Desolina dined alone in a corner. She upset her table-mates with her fidgety behavior. Between courses, she had a compulsion to rearrange things: shift the salt and pepper shakers around, shuffle packets of Sweet-N-Low, and pop the lid up and down on the creamer. The other reason she ate solo was that she was not sociable. Not only was she going deaf; not only was her English poor; but she looked with suspicion on strangers, which she defined as anyone outside her family.

"*Tutti nasone*," she muttered to my mother. "They're all nosy . . . busybodies."

Residents who'd tried to make conversation with her were given the brush off. My mother once tried to hook her up with a resident who spoke Italian, but the rendezvous was a failure.

Before mealtime, residents would gather on benches outside the dining room. When the doors opened, Desolina would bash through the crowd with her walker, her eyes aimed on her table and the first course awaiting her: steaming soup, coleslaw, or Jell-O salad. After the meal, she found her way back to her room, where she watched TV, waited for an aide to give her a bath or change her linens and, literally, twiddled her thumbs.

My father had tried talking her into taking an arts and crafts class. No interest.

Attending an ecumenical religious service.

No.

The final try was an exercise class held in a common room. Desolina stood at the threshold, watching an assemblage of her cohorts spinning their arms, twirling their ankles, and doing neck circles. Some stood, others were in wheelchairs. Marching music played.

She turned to my father and said, "*Ma, cosa fanno queste sciocchi?* What are these foolish people doing?"

"CHE COSA VUOI CHE FACCIO?!"

"*Che cosa vuoi che faccio?!*" my father hollered. "Huh, Mama?! What do you want me to do?!"

He knew what she wanted. I knew what she wanted. Even a man visiting his ailing wife seated near us knew what Desolina wanted, and he didn't speak a word of Italian.

Desolina wouldn't say it. She knew what the answer would be. She wanted to go and live with my father.

A year after Tony's death, she had slipped in the dining room and fractured her hip. She was ninety-five and in good health and was given an artificial hip. It was amazing to think of that piece of technology planted into a body that had come into the world under the care of a midwife.

Now came the hard part: physical therapy. The hospital had released her not to the pleasant surroundings of Director's Hall, where residents had to be fully ambulatory, but into a nursing home, where patients, lined up in wheelchairs against the walls, babbled all day. My grandmother detested the place, but could not return to her apartment until she could walk. She didn't want to do the therapy. She wanted to toss in the towel and move in with my father.

It was an impossible proposition. She needed round the clock care.

"*Mama, che cosa vuoi che faccio?*" my father asked again. She was sitting in a wheelchair in an atrium. The floor nurse had told us that her therapy was not going well. Desolina wasn't cooperating.

"You've abandoned me here," she said, in Italian, starting to whimper.

"Mama, I've told you a hundred times. It's not me who made you come here. It's your doctor. When you're walking again, you can go back to the other place."

Desolina waved that notion away. "Why do I have to learn to walk again?! I'm an old woman!"

My father bit his lower lip so hard I was afraid he'd draw blood. He turned to me for help. I was the grandson, whom Desolina and Antonio had spoiled as a boy. My youth brought sunshine into their lives. Most importantly, my grandmother and I didn't share an entangled history.

"Nonna, what he says is right," I said. "All you have to do is listen to the nurses . . ."

Desolina had no interest in my opinion; she was fighting for her life. She gave me a glare that produced goose bumps on the back of my neck.

Desolina did not want to accept that in American society most adult children didn't give their parents twenty-four hour care; they sent them to assisted living communities and nursing homes.

What made the home arrangement truly impossible was their complex relationship. My father was an only child and, since his youth, Desolina had insinuated herself into his life. She doted on him as a boy; tried to rein him in as a teenager; chastised him for moving away from her as an adult. He was her world. In my father's eyes, her love and affection—and what she passed off as love and affection—were suffocating. Her moving in was out of the question: Mother and son hadn't lived under the same roof since he was twenty-two, and he wasn't going to allow it four decades later.

"*Mama, che cosa vuoi che faccio?*" My father wiped his brow with a handkerchief.

It was 10 a.m. We were sitting in a sunny atrium, Desolina in a wheelchair staring at her shoes.

"What do you do all day?!" she asked. "You're retired!"

"Semi-retired," my father shot back.

"Why do you still have to work? Don't you have enough money in the bank?" she asked sarcastically.

My father looked away and shook his head in disgust.

"There was money when Papa died!" she continued.

"He left it to you," my father countered.

The man near us was shifting uncomfortably. Even his wife, who seemed to have Alzheimer's, looked alarmed at the scene.

Feeling helpless, my grandmother attacked.

"As soon as Papa died, you deserted me!" she cried. "You put me in this zoo!"

My father's face reddened; veins on his neck appeared. His eyes looked as if they would pop out of their sockets. I was afraid he was going to have a stroke and that my grandmother would get her wish: To spend her last days with him, though the two of them would be living side by side in a nursing home instead of his condominium.

He was torn in half: The voice from the Old Country told him that good sons knuckled under to their mother's demands; the voice of the New World insisted that she was responsible for her own life.

"I have no friends here!" she said.

Getting no response, she said, "If your father was alive he'd be ashamed of you, leaving me in a place like this. Maybe you just want his money!"

It was her last broadside—an attempt to deflate his honor, not to mention his masculinity which, poor woman, was how her overbearing love also affected him. He stood up from his chair with the clearest of eyes.

"You don't wanna walk again, Mama? You don't have to. As far as I am concerned, you can stay here for the rest of your life!" he yelled gesturing towards the slumping souls in their wheelchairs. "It's not my fault that you're here. You broke your hip. You can get up and go back to Director's Hall or I'll visit you here for the rest of your life—while you stare at the walls!"

She looked up at the two of us with hate-filled eyes and then, in a kind of Old Testament gesture of futility, stuck a hand in her mouth and bit it.

We turned around and left. We got into my father's Cadillac. After wiping tears from our eyes, he jumped on the gas and screeched out of the parking lot. As we turned onto the main road, we passed the solarium of the nursing home. In a picture forever frozen in my mind, Desolina was sitting in her wheelchair with her face buried in her hands

But walk again she did. Desolina returned to Director's Hall, and continued to take second and third helpings of food. Over time, she mellowed. With the staff, she became charming and easy going. My father was less in her pull. Her memory, which had rested on shaky foundations since her seventies, slowly failed. She completely forgot about New York. It was as if Hell's Kitchen and Astoria had never existed. Her mind was increasingly filled with images of her youth. She talked about brothers and sisters and noted the exact dates of their deaths. She began singing love songs in Italian, some of which were bawdy.

The months passed. My mother visited daily, my father on Sunday.

"A beautiful place and the food is delicious," Desolina reported at the beginning of every visit. "*Ma, chi paga?*"

FINE

Two months before her 97th birthday, Desolina broke her other hip. She survived the surgery, but not the recovery. She was laid to rest in a mid-priced casket from a funeral home with a colonial facade and Chippendale roof in Kalamazoo. The following mourners were present: my father and mother, my two siblings and myself, my father's cousin, Italo Alblondi, who flew up from Washington, D.C., and my mother's cleaning lady. Desolina, the last of nine siblings, had outlived just about everyone who knew her. We called a niece back in Italy, told her to spread the word.

Desolina was laid out in a favorite dress. Missing from her face were her cat-eye glasses. Strung around her fingers—by the funeral director who knew nothing about her indifference to the Catholic Church—was a rosary. We invented our own service: a string of reminiscences and a few readings from—among all things—The Book of Common Prayer. Then we brought her to the cemetery to lay her next to my grandfather, in a location she would have loved: on top of a hill, backed by a forest, and within sight of a pond. She had once told my father not to bury her near a noisy freeway, as many of her friends were, or, worse, in a low-lying area.

"È troppo umido li," she said. "It's too humid there."

We got out of the limousine to stand by the grave. It was strange to see

VESCOVI
ANTONIO DESOLINA

carved in stone in a cemetery in Michigan. They rest among the descendants of Dutch colonists, whose tombstones have interlocking hearts, flowers, and greeting-card poetry. Desolina's and Tony's is as they lived: square and simple.

When we arrived home from the cemetery, my father opened the mail to find paperwork approving Desolina for Medicaid. In the months preceding her death, he had spent tens of hours getting the forms right, coaxing her for a signature, obtaining stamps from the Italian government, and dealing with "the blithering idiots who overpopulate the government."

He tossed the paperwork to me.

"See, she did this. She died on me the day her Medicaid went through. She knew it all along."

On one of my visits to the apartment in Astoria, I arrived to find Tony in poor shape. I called my father, and he flew in early the next day. He burst into the apartment. His terrified eyes searched for his father, who was lying on the couch. He rushed over to Tony, who scolded my father for coming, even as the geriatric ward at Astoria General was awaiting his arrival.

My father stood up and turned around. Desolina was seated at the table, rocking back and forth and simpering. I suspect she thought she deserved my father's first attentions for all her mental anguish. Instead, his glance shifted from her to me. He walked over and, with tears flooding his eyes, said, "I don't know what I'd do without you." We embraced while Desolina continued to gnash her teeth.

How effortless it had been: I gave him a gift simply by virtue of being a grandson.

I now feel a sense of relief. Tony's fine. Desolina rests in peace. Their stories are written down. My children still talk about kicking the plastic fruit around their apartment. And my father sleeps easy at night.

"When I go to the cemetery," he says, "I talk to both of them."

—END—

RECIPES

Neither Desolina, nor my mother's mother, Dirce Pasquinelli, were people comfortable with pencil and paper. For the most part, they did not keep recipes. If you asked Dirce what went into her "piano," the stuffing for tortellini, she'd say, with her characteristic impatience, "Va te maladisa! A little of this, a little of that! Don't bother me!"

My mother and my wife pieced together these recipes for some of the family's favorite dishes. Enjoy.

TURTEI (dialect for tortelli or ravioli)
Traditionally a mix of greens, usually Swiss chard, spinach and beet tops, but any mix of comparable seasonal greens—peasant foods are practical, if nothing else, as well as resilient and forgiving. These are exactly the qualities you gain when you eat turtei!

Take about:

1 and 1/2 pounds of 3 or more mixed greens
4 tablespoons of butter or butter and olive oil mixed
2 nice sized shallots, thinly sliced (shallots are the most nutritious and least subject to molds of all the onions)
Chopped herbs such as parsley or basil or both equaling about ¼ cup
1/2 cup of a soft cheese like ricotta, mascarpone or even cream cheese in a pinch (bring down its sweetness with a little sprinkle of salt)
1/2 lb. of fresh grated Parmigiano-Reggiano
1 egg
Salt and pepper always. It's good to know that sea salt is actually a low sodium salt with high trace minerals that is very beneficial for energy.

Tear off greens from stems. It's easy and satisfying to simply rip the leaf away from the stem or any of the tougher ribs. Wash greens and toss dripping into a wide pan. This water will serve to steam them and cook them down, about 8 to 10 minutes. Drain under cold water to retain intense color. Then squeeze excess water out of the greens; do this playfully, but reverently. They have just given their lives for you. Now chop them in ribbons of 1-inch wide. Mix cheese, egg, herbs, salt and pepper. Set aside.

Now you can make the pasta dough.

Classic Egg Pasta Dough

3 cups of flour turned out onto a table or board in mounded shape; press bottom of small bowl into top of mound to make a well in the center.

Now comes the fun part.

Break 4 eggs into the well. Stop and observe the humor of it. Four eyes will be looking up at you with trust. With a fork, and working quickly, scrape flour from the inside well into the eggs, lightly and little by little. Once the eggs are absorbed by the flour, you may now push the rest of the flour into the mess and begin to knead about 10 minutes until smooth and elastic. If it is sticky add a little more flour. Be patient and strong. Wrap it in cloth or plastic and set it rest for 10 to 30 minutes. You rest, too. You will want to perfect this technique before you invite observers, but you will master it quickly. From now on you will never do it any other way; it's magical.

Divide the dough into two balls (easier to handle by divide and conquer) and roll out as thinly as possible on a floured surface. Then working from the center outwards, turn it like a clock, keep pressing from center outwards, keep turning, and rolling till you are tired. Your second ball is of course covered and waiting in the wings.

Cut your dough into strips. Some edges, of course, will be curved, but don't worry about this, the universe takes care of it. Now back to the filling. The amount of filling you drop onto the pasta is your choice—a tablespoon is good, but leave enough dough between fillings to cut them into pillows, once you cover them with the second sheet of dough.

Now from a separate small bowl of one egg yolk beaten with a few drops of water, brush (or you can use the back of a spoon dipped in the binder) around the filling, apply second sheet of dough on top, press your fingers around filling to seal the pillows and simply cut them apart with a sharp knife or pastry cutter. Move pillows to floured board, cloth or pan, and let the pillows rest for an hour or so. Drop them into boiling, lightly salted for 3 to 4 minutes, then drain. Melt 4 tablespoons of butter with 4 small sage leaves torn to bits and tossed into the butter. Pour butter into a beautiful serving bowl and fold in Turtei. Sprinkle with about half a cup of Parmigiano-Reggiano.

Carry out the bowl in both hands held high above your head. Land on table with ceremony.

ANULIN (known widely as cappelleti—little caps—in broth)

Old style with short cut annotations:

Anulin is that intense, comforting chicken broth with bobbing little chicken stuffed packets for amplified flavor. It can be made by hand at each stage, or helped along by purchased products, but either way, you will recover from whatever ails you. Make it with love and serve it on the weekends to bring release, sustenance, and family feeling.

Take about:

4 tablespoons of butter
1/2 a medium onion, chopped (shallots are even better)
1 celery rib finely chopped
1/2 pound of cooked chicken meat (old style would come from chicken from your homemade stock, while a short cut would be meat from a rotisserie chicken)
1/2 cup of mascarpone, or ricotta
1/2 cup freshly grated Parmigiano-Reggiano
2 tablespoons finely chopped fresh parsley
2 eggs

Sauté onion and celery in 2 tablespoons of butter until translucent. Stir in chopped, warming nicely, then add about 1/4 cup of broth
Cover and let simmer for about 10 minutes. Remove pan from heat, let cool enough to transfer to bowl and mash with fork (Old Style) or in food processor (do not overprocess). Mix in cheese, parsley and an egg, salt and pepper to taste.

Time to make the dough (see previous pages). When you've rolled it out, continue with directions below.

Drop about 1/2 teaspoon of your chicken filling in one row at one edge of the dough in one-inch increments. You are going to flip this edge over your filling, so the fold touches the filling. But first take your egg wash and paint around the filling, then take your dough and fold it over, pressing the dough around the mounds to seal. Cut between the mounds either with a sharp knife or a cookie cutter, and trim if you feel like it. Now lay your beauties on floured pan or cutting board. Admire. This is essential to this recipe. Call someone in to come and look at them. Repeat your technique for the second row, now that you have the hang of it.

Bring 4 quarts of lightly salted water (now that you know the proper finger pinch) to a boil in a pot and bring the broth to a simmer in a second pot. Lovingly drop your anulini into the boiling water. As soon as they rise to the surface, transfer them with a strainer into the broth and cook until al dente, about 6 to 8 more minutes. Serve with a generous dash of olive oil into center of bowl.

TORTA Back in Italy, everyone brought her prize version of this dish to the sagre (plural of sagra). After the immigrants arrived in the United States, in lieu of the sagre, they maintained their communal bonds by meeting annually at dinner galas. These events were largely potluck and, at the Bercetese galas in New York City in the 1930s, torte varieties included savoy cabbage, spinach, zucchini and even rice.

2 1/2 pounds of russet potatoes, scrubbed, leave skin on
6 tablespoons butter
2 small shallots
2/3 cups washed and chopped leek
1/2 cup plus 2 tablespoons mascarpone, or ricotta
2/3 cup freshly grated Parmigiano-Reggiano
3/4th cup cream or milk
Salt and pepper
2 large eggs
Torte dough (recipe follows)

Cut potatoes in half, toss in bowl with 2 tablespoons of oil, 1 tablespoon chopped herbs of choice, and 1 tablespoon sea salt. Roast on baking pan at 425 degrees for 20-30 minutes until tender. While potatoes are roasting, sauté shallots with leeks in butter until soft, but not brown. In a bowl, mix shallots and leeks, cheeses, cream or milk, salt and pepper. When potatoes are cooled, mash with fork or food processor, add eggs, process lightly, and add all ingredients together. This mix can be made a day early, too.

Torte dough. It is a simple, comforting activity.

Handle the dough lightly, with humor, sing to it, but not too much:

2 cups flour
1/2-teaspoon salt-if you pinch salt between your thumb and first two fingers and toss it over flour, even better
1/2 cup plus 1 tablespoon of warmish water
4 Tablespoons plus 1/2-teaspoon olive oil

Mix flour and salt first, then pour in water, then oil. If you can, wheel bowl by placing one hand on the outside and turning, while mixing liquids with fork or fingers. You'll feel at one with the dough. Otherwise, just fork it, but quit as soon as you sense it's uniform. Let it rest for 20 minutes or even overnight so it can collect itself.

Divide the dough in two parts. Roll out one dough on floured surface as thin as you can possibly make it—give yourself ahead of time the knowledge that it will take coaxing. You will taste it later. There will be a moment, about 4 minutes in, when the dough seems to warm up and relax. Then it can really start to stretch out. Lay it upon a walled baking dish or torte pan leaving an overhang of about 2 inches. Shape it into the pan with a light hand. You can transfer dough with some clever tricks: slide a flexible cutting board you've lightly dusted with flour, under the dough, or roll out on flowered tablecloth to begin with, then you can just roll it up, and unroll it over the pan (this technique is a little harder to work with, but great for showoffs). Now fill your dough-lined dish with the torte mix, spreading evenly. Roll out your second ball of dough and top the mix pressing or rolling edges together to seal in filling for baking. Pierce top of dough with knife to allow steam to escape and trim edges. Baste the top and edges lightly with a pastry brush dipped in milk. Bake in pre-heated oven at 425 degrees until golden brown, around 35 to 50 minutes depending on depth of pan. Turn oven temp lower if you feel it is baking too hot. Let it cool before cutting.

Making torte and sharing it wins you a place with the angels.

SCRAPBOOK

Selvi Vescovi and his parents in 1940.

The author and his grandparents at his graduation Columbia University in 1984, when he earned a degree in "extra college."

Tony, Selvi, and Desolina at the author's wedding in 1987.
The photo was taken before Tony consumed several double Scotches.

On the stoop in Astoria in 1992 are (left to right) James, Tony, Luca
(also known as "Il Boy"), the author's brother Mark, and Desolina.

Desolina at her 91st birthday party. Bacci a tutti.

For more photos and stories, visit www.eatnowtalklater.com. At that site, you can listen to the author reading some of the stories as well.